Windows into the Soul

Windows into the Soul

ART AS SPIRITUAL EXPRESSION

Michael Sullivan

MOREHOUSE PUBLISHING

Harrisburg, Pennsylvania

Morehouse Publishing, P.O. Box 1321, Harrisburg, PA 17105

Morehouse Publishing, 445 Fifth Avenue, New York, NY 10016

Morehouse Publishing is an imprint of Church Publishing Incorporated.

Cover design by Lee Singer

Library of Congress Cataloging-in-Publication Data

Sullivan, Michael, 1966 Nov. 20-
 Windows into the soul : art as spiritual expression / Michael Sullivan.
  p. cm.
 ISBN 0-8192-2127-9 (pbk.)
 1. Prayer—Christianity. 2. Spiritual life—Christianity. 3. Christianity and art. 4. Sullivan, Michael, 1966 Nov. 20- I. Title.
 BV215.S835 2006
 246—dc22

                        2005031173

Printed in the United States of America

06 07 08 09   10 9 8 7 6 5 4 3 2 1

For Page, my beloved wife and best friend, who has helped me notice and open more windows than anyone else on the journey

WINDOWS INTO THE SOUL
Art as Spiritual Expression

explorefaith.org books: An Introduction x

Introduction xiii

OPENING THE WINDOWS: A Guide for the Journey 1

WINDOW ONE: Letting God Have It 11
Prayer One: Word Collage 14

WINDOW TWO: Unlearning Prayer 17
Prayer Two: Mixed Media 18

WINDOW THREE: Creating Holy Space 25
Prayer Three: Creating Your Altar to God 28

WINDOW FOUR: Praying Each Day 33
Prayer Four: Mandalas 34

WINDOW FIVE: Surprised by Miracles 39
Prayer Five: Milagros and Intercessory Prayer 42

WINDOW SIX: Living in the Moment 45
Prayer Six: Word Collage II 47

WINDOW SEVEN: Reconciling the Internal and External 51
Prayer Seven: Self-Portrait 53

WINDOW EIGHT: Seeking Forgiveness 57
Prayer Eight: Mixed Media Self-Portrait 59

WINDOW NINE: Getting to the Cross 63
Prayer Nine: Finding Your Cross 65

WINDOW TEN: Finding the Empty Tomb 69
Prayer Ten: Pictures of Life and the Love of God 71

THE OPEN WINDOW: The Final Medium 75

Appendix 81
Small Group Study 81
Preparing for Individual Confession 85

explorefaith.org books
an introduction

The book you hold in your hand says a lot about you. It reflects your yearning to forge a deep and meaningful relationship with God, to open yourself to the countless ways we can experience the holy, to embrace an image of the divine that frees your soul and fortifies your heart. It is a book published with the spiritual pilgrim in mind through a collaboration of Morehouse Publishing and the website explorefaith.org.

The pilgrim's path cannot be mapped beforehand. It moves toward the sacred with twists and turns unique to you alone. Explorefaith.org books honor the truth that we all discover the holy through different doorways, at different points in our lives. These books offer tools for your travels—resources to help you follow your soul's purest longings. Although their approach will change, their purpose remains constant. Our hope is that they will help clear the way for you, providing fruitful avenues for experiencing God's unceasing devotion and perfect love.

www.explorefaith.org
Spiritual Guidance for Anyone
Seeking a Path to God

A non-profit website aimed at *anyone* interested in exploring spiritual issues, explorefaith.org provides an open, non-judgmental, private place for exploring your faith and deepening your connection to the sacred. Material on the site is rich and varied, created to highlight the wisdom of diverse faith traditions, while at the same time expressing the conviction that through Jesus Christ we can experience the heart of God. Tools for meditating with music, art, and poetry; essays about the spiritual meaning in popular books and first-run films; a daily devotional meditation; informative and challenging responses to questions we have all pondered; excerpts from publications with a spiritual message—all this and more is available online at explorefaith.org. As stated on the site's "Who We Are" page, explorefaith.org is deeply committed to the ongoing spiritual formation of people of all ages and all backgrounds, living in countries around the world. The simple goal is to help visitors navigate their journey in faith by providing rich and varied material about God, faith, and spirituality. That material focuses on a God of grace and compassion, whose chief characteristic is love.

You have the book, now try the website. Visit us at www.explorefaith.org. With its emphasis on God's infinite grace and the importance of experiencing the sacred, its openness and respect for different denominations and religions, and its grounding in the love of God expressed through Christianity, explorefaith.org can become a valued part of your faith-formation and on-going spiritual practice.

Introduction

I remember well the last time I saw Abbie. She was sitting at a table in the church basement covered in paint from her hands to her elbows. Painting her latest creation in clay, she was the image of eighteen-year-old perfection: blond, glistening hair falling down in curls that made faithless boys believe, a large smile with perfect, white, shimmering teeth, and a passion for life that intoxicated everyone around. She assaulted life with a love that her contemporaries savored and adults admired. She was athletic yet graceful, beautiful yet ordinary. She was heading to college in the fall and she couldn't wait to expand her horizons in God's great world.

That last time I saw her she was so mesmerized by painting that she didn't notice the mess she was making. Paint in her hair, on the table, and all over her clothes, she was in her element. Creating, dreaming, and playing all rolled into one, she was an incredible mass of energy and fire that captured everyone in the room. Others were saying, "Look out, Abbie, you're getting paint in your hair," or, "Abbie, don't get the glaze on the table." But Abbie just kept going. She was glazing her sculpture and nothing was interfering with her quest to get it just right, to express something deep within, something so many of her friends had already forgotten and which so many adults spend lifetimes trying to capture every now and then. She was catching the creativity of Andy Warhol in color and whim, and the spiritual connectedness of Michelangelo and da Vinci. She was in the basement of a church expressing her deepest thoughts, hopes, and dreams, and she loved it. The person within was finding her way into the world.

One week later on a Friday afternoon, the phone rang. My wife answered and in an instant my world stopped. Even before she spoke, I felt the air in my lungs escaping, the blood in my veins rushing, my eyes swelling with tears. "There's been an accident," she said. Abbie was dead. Abbie and her best friend, Molly, had been killed in a freak boating accident. Two girls left school for "seniors' day off" and died just seventeen years into life. A whole town began to cry.

Everyone who has experienced the unexpected death of a loved one knows the feelings of the next days. Horror mixes with anger, shock blends with fright, and sadness shakes with fear. Floods of tears, nervous chatter, uncontrollable energy, and inexhaustible exhaustion mix together in a horrible combination of gut-wrenching angst.

I was tortured by these feelings. While I let others see my pain and inability to cope with the loss, I didn't let them—or even myself—into my sadness. I was so captured by the grief of others that I didn't take the time to feel my own despair.

For many nights after the girls' deaths I sobbed into my pillow. I knew the tears were bringing me closer to the loss that death inflicts on us but I really had no idea how very depressed I was. I had stuffed the deaths of Abbie and Molly down deep and had expected the loss to lie fallow in the recesses of my soul. But the more I pushed the deaths away, the more intensely the darkness pervaded my soul. I had no idea how, but I knew I had to claw my way out of a growing dark abyss.

For several years, I had sculpted and dabbled in art. I knew that signs, symbols, and metaphors of art could free the soul. Art helped me to explore places within that I had never imagined or acknowledged—creative places where the person in me burst out in new songs with words and phrases only I knew but with melodies that others seemed to understand. Being creative with art allowed me to let go of inhibitions and embrace a radical love of God's creation and my place in it as a beloved creature.

God's calling in art brought a freedom that I had not previously experienced. Earlier in my spiritual life, I had fallen subject to what we might call the consumerism of American religion. If I needed God more, I needed God as a good—God as an object available from the nearest inspirational shelf. If my faith was lacking, I filled the void with something to aid my walk in faith—a new Bible, cross, picture, anything new. I had learned to consume as a release from all that bothered me, so filling my life with spiritual things was also a way to con myself into "feeling better" spiritually.

But such a God hadn't worked. Several years before the girls' deaths, dark problems emerged in my family and consumption-based spirituality failed me. Bouts with cancer and substance abuse in those I loved made the thing I called God irrelevant. My God was broken and there was no use in buying a new one. If God were to help me recover from life—or rather, if I were to start living with God and for God—then God had to be real. My God had to deal with the pain and suffering, the dark and dirty secrets, the horrible midnights that visited humanity, the haunting dreams that visited me.

Having begun a trek of discovery and literally throwing away my God while praying for a rebirth, I set out on a course of reading. I read every spiritual book available. I tried the classics of evangelicals and the cryptic clamorings of mystics and poets. From time to time I would land on something that inspired me, something that burst God wide open and made God relevant. Those glimpses of God usually occurred with the poet Eliot or Auden close at hand.

What was happening, although I didn't know it, was that I was embarking on a journey with Abraham and Sarah, David, Ruth, James, and John. I was leaving behind a scientific approach to my faith, where things had to be black and white, and entering a cloud of unknowing, where metaphor and imagination were not only possible but celebrated. And more importantly, I was getting ready to hear God's poetry and see God's canvas for the very first time. God the scientist was dying; God the poet and artist was coming into view.

The breakthrough came during a workshop on spirituality. I was assigned to a studio arts class one afternoon. The leader took one look at me and declared, "You have the hands of a sculptor." Thinking this new-age guru was off her rocker, I scoffed at first but took the large lump of clay she handed me. Within minutes of touching that cold, clammy lump of earth I knew she was right. I couldn't get enough of working with clay. Sculpting touched my soul in a way that nothing else ever had. I felt alive, independent, and resourceful—yet vulnerable, dependent, and connected.

But more importantly, the process opened me to the possibility of a God I couldn't understand or contemplate. I began to discover a peace I'd never known. I began to engage myself with God not as object but with God who was happy to be subject—subject to all the world could throw, torture, trouble, or tempt. The process of sculpting opened me to a God who made sense to me precisely because I couldn't understand God. This was a God who would take on what I experienced, take on what my life brought, and push through it all to find light. This was a God who was relevant.

And so art became the vehicle of my prayer. It provided a framework for going within, for exploring places and feelings I would otherwise just stuff deeper and deny. Being creative with art allowed me to find a safe place to probe how the pains of life played out in my ordinary life and to re-clothe myself with creativity and freedom. It provided a place to be the person God created me to be.

But when Abbie and Molly died, so did the art and prayer. Nothing worked. Sculpting was so very painful. When I would sit down, all I could think about was the pain and the suffering—not only mine, but the pain of the whole town. Art became a chore and the freedom I normally found was gone. Thinking I'd just lost touch with my creativity, I started concentrating on technique. But that made me less of a praying artist and more a practicing one. Art became a craft. I couldn't connect the art with my feelings and with God. God started to feel black and white again.

Then, one sunny afternoon when I was laboring with another sculpture-going-nowhere I remembered Abbie's pieces, the ones she'd glazed just days before her death. I ran to them, carefully touching the creations of a girl I couldn't have imagined life without. I began to cry. I was holding the soul of another, a loved one, and from the depth of her being, she was speaking to me. She was asking me to let go

I took Abbie's pieces to the kiln. Opening the heavy lid and reaching down into the brick oven, I could feel the weight of Abbie as I placed the pieces into the kiln. I didn't want to leave them there; I didn't want to leave *her* there. Letting go took time—several hours, really. But as I closed the kiln and started that long process of heat, fire, and purification, I realized that Abbie herself had already let go.

I watched each stage of firing in utter amazement over the next two days. I'd seen firings many times before. I knew what to do and how to do it. But this time was different. At each stage of the process, I peered into the side of the kiln, looking deep into its fire as the temperature rose higher and higher. I saw Abbie's small bowl and cup whiten and glisten in the heat until at the highest temperatures they faded completely into the heat themselves, becoming one with the kiln somewhere around two thousand degrees. They disappeared into an orange and red purification only to emerge a couple of days later beautiful, colorful, vibrant, and strong. The kiln, which burned away Abbie's last human touch, transformed and purified her prints into resurrected caresses of divine hands. Out of the death, Abbie's creation burst forth with new life.

A couple of days later, I took the pieces to Abbie's parents. I'll never forget how I felt walking up to their front door. Despite the pain the community had known, none of us knew the loss that both Abbie's and Molly's parents had endured. I wanted to run away. I wanted more than anything to flee from the pain and loss. But I also wanted to live into the hope of those resurrected pieces from the kiln, and having seen that life, I surely wanted to share it with her parents.

When her parents opened the box and pulled the small bowl from the tissues, tears flowed out of us like mountain streams after a storm. We sat there on a beautiful summer day weeping as we held those gorgeous pieces from Abbie, those testimonies of her life in the midst of our grieving. Through her creation, we heard her prayer and saw her life. Her lyrical prayer was embodied within the form, and while we couldn't fully understand, we experienced a melody of love, beauty, and peace. From that moment, art not only played a role in my own journey, I knew it had to play a journey in all our lives. There had to be a way to translate what I'd experienced in art so that others could experience this transformation and rebirth as well. Abbie's gift was not just a couple of pieces of ceramic created in a church basement. Abbie's gift was a path to life.

This book is about finding that pathway. The art we encounter will help you connect with God by opening up your prayer life and deepening your own faith. It is my hope that in the pages of this book you, too, will benefit from Abbie's gift and find, through creativity, your own path to life and God.

Opening the Windows
A Guide for the Journey

Put me to the test, says the Lord of hosts; see if I will not open the windows of heaven for you and pour down for you an overflowing blessing.

Malachi 3:10

The chapters in this book open windows to the soul by mapping the pathways between art and prayer. Cultivating the creative spirit opens a place of freedom and vulnerability in us and we become willing to pray. Then, and only then, do we really communicate with God or become aware that God is communicating with us. But the method is not just for the tried-and-true believer. While it's certainly for those who have never strayed from organized religion, it is also applicable to those who doubt and question all that churches offer. Seekers and believers will both find new life within these exercises.

The method I recommend combines artistic expression with soul-searching. We delve into the dark recesses of who we are in order to see how God wants to cast light into our darkness. Art allows this process to take on a physical form that is often missing from typical prayer life. By jumping into the exercises, we find ways to express our innermost thoughts and feelings. These exercises encourage your soul to take flight among the things that enslave you. They form windows to the soul—places where, despite the dark panes of life, God invites you to see through a glass more clearly. They ask you to yell, scream, poke, and prod the God you call Christ so that God's life might be yours as you pray. They ask you to laugh, joke, and celebrate the Jesus who so loves you and this world by inviting you to all the crucifix-

1

ions, resurrections, and ascensions of life—the opportunities to experience the reconciling love of God by letting God have it—by letting God have it all.

Before continuing, I offer some practical suggestions to guide your journey. While the rest of the book takes you step by step into a deeper awareness of prayer and God's faithfulness, here are tips that I think you'll find helpful as you embark upon the journey.

Generate honesty, not masterpieces.

This book won't make you into a professional artist. You won't learn how to paint, draw, or sculpt, though you may stumble upon great talent and unearth a masterpiece as you go through the exercises. Be open to that possibility but don't set yourself up for disappointment. These projects are about connecting with God more deeply, not about producing world-class art.

Likewise, this book won't make you a professional at prayer. I'm not so sure there is such a thing—or that there ought to be. Instead, allow the artistic process help you to get you in touch with being a plain old human being. Don't focus on technicalities—just let the freedom of the journey take you to a place of discovery where your soul is able to be itself. Don't worry about artistic methods, whether you're painting "correctly" or sculpting with expertise. Don't worry about prior experience. Don't even think about talent. Instead, seek a pathway in art that connects you to prayer, and ultimately, to God. Let go of any preconceived notions of what art and prayer are all about and just let the process evolve. If you can do that and focus on the creative space that opens when you enter meditation and contemplation, you might create a masterpiece and end up praying honestly.

Put criticism aside.

Sometimes the voices of critique within all of us are persistent. I've found two approaches that help me silence those voices.

The first method involves visualization. Try to identify the critical voice you hear as you pray. Do you hear a particular person's voice or is it more of an abstract feeling? Identify it, then, visualize it and place it in the palm of your hand. Then take that criticism and place it on the canvas, clay, or whatever medium you're working with. You won't actually draw, cut, or sculpt this criticism. Just imagine that you can put it to the side and let go of it. It's amazing what a simple visualization technique like this can do for you.

If the voice is a person you can't identify, you might try writing words or phrases that describe the critic, using a post-it note or paper and tape. Place the notes on the side of the space in which you're working and just let them be there. I think you'll find this practice liberating. Instead of pushing the critic away completely, this method lets you place the criticism in a safe place, somewhere with a clear boundary around it, and then return to it later if you choose to. Most of the time I find that the criticism wasn't important, but occasionally, I identify a deep issue that I need to consider in my prayer life.

The second strategy for silencing those critical voices works when the criticism will not stop. When that happens, I simply let the critic talk. I stop what I'm doing, listen, and let the voice become a part of the process. This step is more challenging because the boundary isn't distinct and the critic can jump right into the midst of the creative process and stay there. But I usually find that these persistent critics need to be heard if liberation is to come at all. Without listening, the criticism stays below the surface and stifles true creativity, in much the same way my internal critics prevented me from sculpting after Abbie and Molly died. A deep, abiding issue was at hand and the longer I put it away without dealing with it, the less creativity I had, and more importantly, the less I was able to pray.

Get rid of distractions; make space for the journey.

As you place the critics aside or listen to them to go deeper into prayer, also place distractions aside. It's the only way to create holy space for your journey.

You know the challenges. You finally find time to pray. You make an appointment with God and stick to it. You sit down in your chair, turn the radio and TV off, breathe deeply, close your eyes, and just like magic—the phone rings. Or you begin your quiet time and the dog starts barking next door. Or the doorbell rings. Or the UPS man arrives with a package to sign for.

Placing critics aside is hard enough. But placing life—with all its distractions—on hold seems next to impossible. But you must. No exceptions. If prayer is important to your life with God, then make it a priority by giving the time wholly to God. Turn off the phone. Close the door to your room— Jesus thought that was a good idea! Be disciplined. Find a time for prayer when the children are in school, playing at the neighbors, or in bed. Tell your spouse to respect your space. Whatever it takes, eke out a prayer time without interruptions.

Why is it so important to create this uninterrupted time? First, if you're like most people, you're so busy that unless you schedule the time, it won't happen. But there's a deeper reason that's directly related to the spiritual journey. The time and space for prayer create the opportunity for the attentiveness to God so essential to the life in prayer. To move from laundry list praying (God, I need this, this, and this) to listening and asking what God is saying to us (even if God is silent), uninterrupted space is an absolute necessity.

As you go deeper into this space with God, you discover more of who God is—and who you are, too. The discovery is not necessarily one of clarity; many times we learn how little we know about God and how few of us actually live with a daily awareness of the divine. But by making room for attentiveness through the creative process, holy space starts to permeate your whole day, not just your isolated prayer time. The dedicated time you devote to prayer allows you to rediscover a place within your being where attention turns from the world and begins to rest in God.

Just think about it this way: How many times have you gone to bed, and lying there, prayed, "God, thank you for this day and for all that you blessed me with in it. Bless Aunt Betty. Be with John in his surgery . . . and I forgot the dry-cleaning, and the kids have a soccer match tomorrow afternoon, and, and, and. . . ." You were well intentioned and you placed your petitions before God with sincerity and faith, but the moment you became distracted, your prayer fell apart. You went in another direction and likely never returned to your prayer. It's a harsh way to look at it, but by not paying attention to God, the prayer became a vehicle for paying more attention to self and what the self needed. Instead of going deeper into prayer with God, listening and asking how God might reveal grace and love, it just became a way to remember what we needed and wanted. The prayer never really got around to being an opportunity for relationship with God. So make an appointment with God. Eliminate as many distractions as possible. Tell your family and friends you're praying. And then listen. Let your attentiveness become the central focus, be ready for discovery, and let God expand the boundaries of your heart.

Go slowly, be gentle, and don't beat yourself up.

The creative process in these exercises is time-consuming and soul-awakening. The process can't be rushed. So don't speed-read this book. If you zip through it in one sitting you'd miss the point entirely. The prayers need time to percolate within you. The exercises cultivate the soul and stir deep feelings into forms you can see and hear, evoking emotions from incredible joy to long-forgotten grief.

So go slowly. Let the exercises take you wherever the Spirit guides you. Sometimes the art will bring you peace; at other times it may bring you agitation or anger. Prayer can touch all of our emotions—and it should! If we are giving all over to God, then expect all of us—the good, the bad, and the ugly—to show up! At times, your prayer may become too intense, so take a few steps back to a more comfortable place. God will be with you each step of the way, whether you're journeying into something wonderful or something surrounded with sadness. Just remember that you are beloved and God will surround you with divine arms of mercy no matter what you tread upon. It is the cross-shaped love of God in Christ that will hold you, and the Easter joy of the empty tomb that will surround you. Wherever you are, trust in God to guide you each step of the way.

Seek professional help when needed.

If these exercises bring repressed memories to the surface, or if you find yourself depressed or anxious, consider seeking professional help. Seeking therapy is not a sign of weakness but of strength. A therapist can provide a useful and healthy relationship in which to discover more of your self and how you relate to God and the world.

Share your prayer life with others.

Just as the disciples were called to support one another in their life of prayer, we too are called to support one another in our spiritual journeys. We need spiritual companions for comfort, assurance, and love. Personally, I need to check in with others for my prayer life to stay vibrant and fulfilling. Sharing our prayer also provides accountability and a check to our excuses not to pray.

You can practice these exercises alone or in small groups. But in the end, you need to share them. For some people, this is easy to do—they might find it perfectly natural to call a friend right after an exercise to discuss the spiritual insights into life and prayer that they've gained. For others, sharing is a lot more difficult. They might wait months before sharing their discoveries, perhaps because they fear judgment or ridicule.

But whatever your inclination, and no matter how long it takes you, sharing is essential on this journey. Our spiritual companions help us see and hear things in our prayer life that we fail to notice. God just likes speaking though others!

Consider a spiritual director.

Working with a spiritual director—a specially trained person who challenges you to seek God in everyday life—is also helpful. Though the concept of spiritual direction has enjoyed a resurgence of interest, it's often misunderstood as therapy. While both the counselor and spiritual director may address the same subject matter, the way each professional works with that information is quite different.

Spiritual directors aren't therapists. Therapists are generally not concerned with the question of where God is in life. Instead, a therapist helps you process the way you move through life and the way the people and events that have shaped your life impact your daily choices. Therapists also help you address more effective ways of responding to the people and events of your world.

Spiritual direction, on the other hand, focuses on helping you find God amidst all the people, places and events of life. Spiritual directors help you hear how God is speaking in your life, even when you fail to notice God. They ask hard questions and remind you of ways to move deeper into prayer.

Spiritual direction and therapy complement each other. You can apply what you've learned in counseling to the question of God's presence in your life and to ways you've acknowledged or ignored that presence. If you're considering spiritual direction, check out the websites for the Shalem Institute (www.shalem.org), Sursum Corda (www.sursumcordasc.org), and Spiritual Directors International (www.sdiworld.org) to find a qualified professional in your area.

Take the chapters in order.

The exercises in this book build on one another. The first ones take small steps and lay a foundation for bolder prayers later on. The first exercises get you in touch with your creativity and help you let go of preconceived notions about prayer while helping you develop the basic skills necessary for the creative process. They teach you how to be attentive to God and yourself throughout prayer. Later exercises move into deeper reflection, in which the creative process and a baseline grounding in one's journey is assumed. Don't start in the middle—or at the end!

Read the chapter before praying.

Since you'll need to be familiar with the technique in each chapter, take time to read the whole chapter before beginning the exercise. This practice will not only allow you to gather supplies and other items in advance, but will also afford you greater freedom in your prayer practice. You won't be consumed by reading the instructions and you'll avoid the temptation to be overly technical during your prayer time.

Find supplies everywhere.

Don't go to the arts store and buy supplies for a professional studio. Instead, visit local craft stores and purchase inexpensive acrylic paints, brushes, paper, and supplies. The less expensive items will work beautifully for our purposes, so don't fall into the temptation to spend more than necessary.

You can also find a surprising number of supplies in thrift shops and at garage sales and church bazaars. Look for wooden boxes, such as cigar boxes, for storage or for a mixed-media piece. You might, for instance, use that old box, rather than brand-new—and costly—poster board or foam core to mount pieces in a collage. Old mugs make great containers for washing brushes, and if you break them, you can work the shards of pottery into mosaics. You might even find old leather-bound books, remove the pages and add blank paper to use as a journal. Just remove the pages and bind your own journal into the cover. The pages you tear out might even make nice additions to a collage. Yard sales are also great places to find leftover latex paints, scrap wood, brushes, and small items that can be incorporated into collages.

You'll also need lots of old magazines to make collages. Your local library is an excellent resource for outdated periodicals. You can also find worn or used Bibles and religious texts, which you'll need for several of the exercises, in libraries and churches. Keep an eye out, too, for church bazaars and annual library sales, which are also good spots for finding such books.

(Be forewarned—the exercises encourage you to cut, tear, or rip some things from religious texts and hymnals. Don't worry—it's okay! You'll be taking verses to express thoughts and feelings in your prayer life. Trust that God will use these holy texts to reveal more to you.)

Most of all, look for objects that speak to you and symbolize some aspect of your spiritual journey. For some, old nails and screws will be synonymous with the journey. For others, feathers and bits of silk or linen will reflect the walk of the soul. Whatever calls your name, from the old discarded window on the street to the leaves of fall, answer.

See art and prayer everywhere.

Unfortunately, most of us have soaked up the cultural norms for religious art. The typical buffet consists of stained glass figures with stoic faces and long, flowing robes; nice Victorian portraits of a blue-eyed Jesus; and a few alphabet soup symbols, mostly Greek. We have so prettified religious art that most of it only presents a picture; it doesn't really say anything and it doesn't open a window in our soul. It just looks nice.

Don't buy into this narrow view. Paul Tillich, one of the twentieth century's most notable theologians, spoke of art as an expression of an ultimate concern.[1] While we might divide art into religious and secular, Tillich argued that modern art expressed the innermost sense of the individual and how the individual relates to the world. He claimed this truth because he believed that today's art is rooted in the same creative spirit that moved over the face of the earth when God called the universe into being. It's this notion of creativity that encouraged Tillich to see art as evidence of the ultimate concern, the power beyond, the God of the universe. Others have called it the spark of the divine, or *scintilla divinitatis* that calls from within all of us. However we understand it, when we explore who we are in God and we

---

1. Carl Michalson, ed., *Christianity and the Existentialists* (New York: Charles Scribner's Sons, 1956), 128–46.

attempt to put it on canvas or paper, we find a method to unlock the creative spirit and, we encounter God's love for us. We find our place of pilgrimage, a safe and holy place where we remember who we are and whose we are.

Such a pilgrimage is one of discipline and devotion, and some will call you crazy for it. Indeed, many in the religious community will challenge the very idea of art and prayer. But until you're willing to find the call to prayer everywhere in the world, you're not seeking the cross of Christ in every place and person you encounter. So as art becomes your journey into prayer, look for artistic expressions everywhere. You'll be surprised by what you see.

Take Abbie's advice.

As Abbie did, let prayer with art help you become like a child again. Let go of all the inhibitions that come with adulthood and enter a space where you're willing to be the person that God sees—messy, vulnerable, beautiful, and redeemed. In scribbles of crayons, brushes of acrylic, chunks of clay, and scraps of paper, take your place as a beloved child of God among the whole of the heavenly hosts as they all work in the grand studio of God's grace.

WINDOW ONE
Letting God Have It

The Lord is near to all who call on him,
to all who call on him in truth.

Psalm 145:18

Letting God have it is our beginning prayer. Telling God off may not sound like praying, and it's probably not the advice you'd expect to hear from a priest. But learning to be honest with God—telling God what you really think, the good and the bad—is essential to the relationship established in prayer. I speak from experience.

Many years ago, as I was going through a transitional time in my life, a beloved priest suggested I yell at God—and I reacted the same way many people do when I give them the same advice in my office today. At thirty, I was getting ready to go to seminary, my parents had just divorced, and my grandmother, who had been the glue of my childhood and the constant peacemaker in our family, died. I was dealing with addiction in a loved one, winding down my law practice, giving up a sizable salary, packing all our belongings, and asking my wife and eighteen month-old daughter to head off to a seminary in the middle of nowhere. In the throes of this amazing call to a new vocation, I should have been ecstatic. Instead, life made no sense and I was terrified by all the changes around me.

I awoke one night horrified by life itself. I remember thinking that I was alone in the world and losing all that was dear to me. For the next several days, I slid into a deep, dark place that I had no idea existed. An abyss had been beckoning from within me, a place paradoxically both haunting and alluring. What I'd embarked on was my first dark night of the soul. All the transitions pulled and pushed me into a place of pain and suffering. I thought there was something so wrong with me that no one could love me, not even God. I didn't love myself. I hated myself and I thought about ending it all.

I didn't realize it at the time, but deep within, I was angry with God for my parents' divorce and for the death of my beloved grandmother. I wanted to yell out my anger but had no idea how to open my soul before God. My heart was closed, my desires were a mystery, and my life was a secret pain that only I knew. Friends and acquaintances suggested various strategies for dealing with the pain, but nothing worked. Exercise didn't help. Meditation was a farce. I couldn't eat. And therapy—what a waste of time. I remember thinking, "How can I bear my soul to this shrink when I don't know what's going on in me, when I am losing everything I've had? How can anyone understand?"

I began to do what I'd always done under high stress: I gave myself a pep talk: Hunker down. Bear it. Grit your teeth. Keep walking. Keep working. It will go away. It will go away.

Thank God I sought the help of my priest. Someone I trusted and who knew me really well, she made the simplest of suggestions: go to church; yell at God. Like Abraham and Sarah, I laughed out loud at the thought of a God so faithful. God wanted me to yell. Right. God was the soft, gentle, shiny thing up there behind the altar rail. God was some disinterested divine being who walked in the garden long, long ago and then left us—left me—here to figure it out. To yell at God implied that God could hear, might actually listen, and might actually care. And even if God could hear me, as any good Southern boy knew, yelling at God was *not* allowed. No way. Absolutely no way. Yell at God—get in trouble. Yell at God—go to hell. It sounded like an invitation from the devil himself.

But my priest was right. I needed to yell at God. It was important, even necessary. Without it, I was going to take up residence in the abyss. And so on a hot Sunday afternoon with no one around, I walked into our big, empty church. Standing there all alone, I thought I might be able to do it. I was sure I could. But in that empty church, looking at that empty cross, I couldn't yell at the Big Old Man. As much as I tried, my throat clenched like a fist and I stood speechless. Speechless. I was in the safest place on earth, before one who loved me like no other, yet I was scared to death. There was no way I could do it. It just wasn't right, not holy, not me.

My priest said to go again. So I did. Five times. And on the sixth trip I began to talk. Actually, I whispered. I thought I had to be polite. I thought I had to use language God would understand—good, holy, clean language. But an interesting thing happened. As I whispered, I began to cry, and the tears liberated me. What started as a cry became a curse, and with a single phrase flowing from my lips, from the depths of my life, I started praying. If you had been a fly on the wall that day, you wouldn't have described my words as prayer. But for the first time in my life, prayer opened up for me like it never had. The words came and I found it easy to talk with God. I poured out my hurt, my distress that God had not saved me from the pains of divorce, death, and addiction. I told God all I was feeling, wanting, and hoping. About an hour later, I was exhausted. I had yelled at God without stopping for sixty good minutes and I was still alive. I was more alive than ever. God was more alive than ever.

I had discovered that telling God off was essential in the midst of all the transitions I was experiencing. Does that make you want to run from the room, or at least put down this book? Usually, people discourage us from telling God how we really feel. But faced with the grief of our lives, most of us must find a place to let God have it so we can give up control and begin to pray. Look at the Psalms. One after another, the psalmists stand before us calling to this place. Consider Psalm 58, decrying the wicked and perverse. The psalmist is so angry that he asks God to break the teeth of the wicked in their mouths, to let them vanish like water that runs off the mountains. Lots of other Psalms take a similar path: Psalms 31, 38, 39, or 44 for starters. Each of them names the anger of the heart and asks why God doesn't answer.

Few of us enter into the prayer of the psalmists—we'd rather stay in control and hold on tightly. But I learned, standing in that empty church, that I had to fall deeply away from God to fall deeply into God. I had to fall into all the things I feared—into the horror and pain. By accepting God's invitation to tell my Creator off and give up control, my soul began to fill with light and I saw it as it really was for the first time. My soul was God's soul—the empty tomb of God's love for me in the death and life of Christ.

Art can open this same window in your soul and bring in resurrecting light. In the safety of your spiritual home—your soul—you can discover God's invitation to prayer, which invites you to open your heart to participate in the divine grace of God's love for you as you fall into the arms of Christ. For some, that might mean delving into pain and suffering. For others, it might mean a totally different path. One woman, for instance, told me during a recent art meditation that she'd never shared her joy with God, letting her soul's thankfulness just rest in God.

No matter which response you experience, art facilitates the opening of the soul's windows and allows your soul to take flight and soar in God's passion. By its very nature, art allows your vulnerability and your joy to come to the surface—literally—on surfaces of paper, canvas, or clay. It's in expressing the darkness and joys of your life that you discover the grace of God's passion—a duet, if you will, of God's suffering and resurrection with you in your life. Art allows you to discover your soul resting in God—your life's melody and the Son's song of redemption interwoven in the harmony and dissonance of your common life. This is the duet that God sings with you when you're wiling to open the windows to your soul, let the light in, and discover that your very life is the empty tomb of grace.

Prayer One: Word Collage

Time Required: 1 hour

Here's a simple first step you'll probably enjoy as we jump into art and prayer. It's useful as a daily "check-in" or when you're having trouble identifying what's going on in your life, so you may want to go back to this exercise again and again.

Opening Prayer

God, thank you for bringing me to a place of hopefulness. Help me to be myself, to let go, and to see you in this prayer. Amen.

Materials

Gather the following materials before you begin this exercise:
- A large piece of construction paper. Buy a pack and select the color that appeals to you just before you begin. If you like this method after a few times, bind the collages together to form a journal. The patterns and themes will be important to revisit as you move deeper into your prayer life.
- Felt-tipped markers or colored pencils.

Prayer Method

- Find a quiet, comfortable place where you feel safe and willing to speak freely to God. You might consider going to an empty church or a garden, or taking a hike into the woods.
- Follow these simple steps.
  - Close your eyes.
  - Breathe deeply, starting from deep within your abdomen and breathing up into your chest, all the way up to your collarbone. See if you can lengthen your breathing so that your inhalation and exhalation are equal, pausing between them for just a couple of seconds. After breathing this way four or five times, let your breath return to normal.
  - Ask God to bless this time and help you be more willing to give yourself over to your Creator.
  - Begin to meditate on this question: What interferes with my relationship with God?
  - As thoughts begin to materialize, take the markers and write down words or phrases that come to mind. Be sure to reserve one of the colors for later in the exercise.
  - Let the thoughts come as fast as they can; don't pause to analyze or judge them. There are no right or wrong words to use when praying with God. Just let your words and thoughts flow. If you show anger, remember that the psalmists did too. If you use strong words, be thankful that God allows you to be honest.
  - Be creative. Write words upside down, diagonally, in a spiral, pattern—however you choose. Begin to let your inner artist come to life.
  - When the thoughts stop coming, look over what you've listed. Are there any themes? Do the themes spur you to consider other thoughts? If so, jot them down on the page.
  - Take a minute or two to relax and live with your responses. Don't judge them. Just live with them.
  - Now, take the colored marker you've reserved and write what comes to mind when you consider God's response to what you've written. Again, be creative. Let God's response be woven into your words —upside down, diagonally, whatever comes to mind. Does

God have doodles to record? Does God respond with whimsical curls and designs?

– If you have trouble imagining God's response, ask yourself what you've been waiting for God to say to you. What would God say if you were playing on the schoolyard together or running a country road side by side? In other words, what would God as friend have to say to what you have discovered?

– When you are finished receiving God's response, take time to look at the collage again. How does it make you feel? Take time to really live with it and let it sink in.

– With your eyes closed, breathe deeply, as you did at the beginning of the exercise. After four or five deep breaths, let your breathing return to normal and say "Amen."

Soul Questions

• Was it easier to identify your feelings than to tell God how you felt? Why or why not?

• What feelings did you experience? Did your feelings change when you considered God's response to what you'd written?

• What surprises came your way?

• What did you learn about your relationship with God?

Tools for the Journey

• Make a list of the times in your life when you've been honest with God. Why was it possible at those times? Any time you hold things back from God, go to this list and see how you not only survived but how you were strengthened.

• Think about your best friend. What makes it possible to be yourself with that person? How could that relationship influence your prayer life with God?

• Write down how you feel each day at the top of a journal page or on the margins of your calendar. Use the writings as a cheat sheet when praying.

WINDOW TWO
Unlearning Prayer

He was praying in a certain place, and after he had finished,
one of his disciples said to him, "Lord, teach us to pray . . . "

Luke 11:1

The road to God is never as straight and smooth as we wish it were. More than once I've been surprised by the wisdom passed along to me from other pilgrims on the path. That's how I discovered that I needed to unlearn some of my prayers. Let me explain.

Many years ago, I traveled to a monastic community for a retreat. I was searching for answers to spiritual bends in the road at that time—especially as they related to my vocation. So, I thought a week of solitude and spiritual direction would help and made my way to Mirfield, a historic monastery in the North of England. I'd long admired the Mirfield Fathers, men of the faith who also lived and worked among the longshoremen of the Docklands in London. They had also been instruments of peace and reconciliation in South Africa long before Apartheid ended. I sensed that these men would help me understand where I was in my journey and what recent rumblings in my soul meant.

I took meals with the community at Mirfield, took lots of walks, reread T. S. Eliot's *Four Quartets* yet again, and sang prayers in the company of the brothers all day long, from far before the sun came up until long after it went down. The discipline with which they sang their praises and laments to God embodied the very pathway of the artist in prayer. In the melodic lines of prayer they found a way to express their souls. It seemed to me the melodies were canvases upon which they painted their life in prayer.

I also visited with Brother Peter, a spiritual director I'd known from my seminary days. I hoped he might point me in the right direction, or have some word of Scripture that would set me on a path toward wholeness. But what he actually had to say surprised me: "Let the prayers of the church be the prayers of the church," he advised me. "Say them without ceasing, but when you turn from them, be present in the moment of the task God sets before you. Let your sculpting be your prayer. Let your painting be your prayer. Let your breath be your prayer. Nothing more. Just be with God."

In other words, Brother Peter told me to unlearn what I knew about prayer. I shouldn't throw the baby out with the bathwater, of course, but I had to expand my experience of prayer beyond the words I read in dusty old books. He was right. I'd discovered enough freedom with God to be able to pray more openly, but mostly I was still praying in the language I thought God wanted to hear. I thought God wanted prayer to sound like the words of Shakespeare or Billy Graham. But all the "thees" and "thous"—and even the campfire-friendly God-as-chum approaches—left me empty. What I'd learned in art hadn't come fully into my life of prayer.

Don't get me wrong. I come from a tradition where written prayers are the mainstay. We need them. I need them. They're not only a part of me, they also tie me to those who have gone before. From the Lord's Prayer to the words of the Book of Common Prayer, prayers from memory are a vital part of who we are as worshipping Christians. But sometimes we can hide in these prayers. If your prayer is only an arrangement of stock phrases, then you're probably not pushing to new depths in your prayer life. We may be using the lovely words of traditional prayers as a way not to tell God where we are in our lives.

The practice described in this chapter helps you examine the words you use, why you use them, and what they really mean to you. It will also allow you to find new ways to express your soul before God, placing your whole person before your Creator.

Prayer Two: Mixed Media

Time Required: 1–2 hours

This prayer identifies stock phrases you use in your prayers while also illustrating how your faith has both helped and hindered your prayer life. It attempts to liberate the words we know by examining the words of your own faith tradition. That way, you make a conscious decision about whether those words enrich your prayer life.

Opening Prayer

God, help me pray with my own words to express my hopes, dreams, and fears. Open my heart to hear your word in new and challenging ways and deliver me from praying to please you only. Amen.

Materials

Gather the following materials before you begin this exercise:

- A worn Bible that you are willing to cut and tear.
- A worn book from your religious tradition that you are also willing to cut and tear. As an Episcopalian, the Book of Common Prayer is always an excellent resource. For Lutherans, the Augsburg Confessions might work; for a Presbyterian, possibly the Westminster Confession; for Catholics, perhaps a missal or a prayer book. If you're not willing to cut the book, use a photocopy for your prayer.
- If you don't have a Bible or book from your religious tradition, collect readings that have been important to you recently and consider making copies of portions of them for use in this exercise.
- You might also gather copies of prayers that have been helpful to you in the past. Are there prayers you associate with a wonderful day or event? Are there prayers that have been painful, even prayers that may have tormented you along your spiritual journey?
- Select magazines that express various aspects of your life in society. If you're a lawyer, for instance, a bar association newsletter might work. If you exercise, consider a running magazine or a periodical focusing on the sport you like. If you're a cook, bring cookbooks, recipe cards, or food magazines to the table. Whatever your interests, bring printed materials you're willing to cut and tear apart.
- Scissors.
- Rubber cement, tape, and, for heavier items, a glue gun.
- Other paper items that are central to your journey in the faith. You might consider making color copies of photographs of your baptism, a special retreat, or individuals important to your journey.

- Other non-paper items that express some aspect of your journey. If you have "relics" of important spiritual times that you could glue onto poster board, gather them if you are comfortable doing so. For example, an old cross necklace or a pendant given to you at a crossroads in your life makes an excellent addition to the mixed-media creation. Your creation will not necessarily be permanent—you can always retrieve the items if you want.
- A piece of poster board. If you have many non-paper items you anticipate affixing, consider purchasing a piece of foam core to use instead of poster board. You can get foam core from a local craft store or frame shop.
- Acrylic paints or felt-tipped markers.

Prayer Method

- Take the Bible and find a story that speaks to you. Cut or tear it from the pages and set it aside. If the whole of the story falls on two back-to-back pages, take the part that you most identify with in your life or photocopy one of the pages and use that.
- If you don't know of a Bible story or can't identify with one, consider other sources. Is there a story from your childhood that still speaks to you today? Have your read a novel or short story recently that spoke to some aspect of your life? If so, make a copy of those pages and use them instead.
- Now take the book from your religious tradition. Without thinking, go through it quickly and when a word or phrase jumps out at you, cut or tear it out and place it to the side. Don't worry if you cut or tear more words than you need. You'll only need a few of them but don't be shy; take whatever reaches out for you. If you identify with it, it's important. Work quickly without pausing to reflect on what the words mean to you or how they reflect your journey. There will be ample time for reflection and discernment later. Just work quickly and continue working until you no longer find words or phrases that pull at you.
- If you don't have a book from your tradition, write words or phrases from your life that point to spiritual understandings and experiences. If you like, write them on sheets of colored construction paper or even print them on the computer.

- Repeat this same process with the magazines from various aspects of your life. Continue to work quickly, taking images and words that jump out at you. Place the cuttings to the side.
- When you've exhausted the process with the magazines, begin to work with the objects from your spiritual journey. If you think of items that hadn't occurred to you earlier, go find them. If you didn't identify any objects before beginning the exercise, consider whether you know of any now.
- Begin arranging these items on the poster board or foam core. Continue to work without reflecting on the items. Let each item speak on its own without considering how it relates to your journey. You're asking God to liberate the experience of prayer, to make it free and open to new experiences and understandings of self and God. You'll also let go of religious and societal expectations about your prayer in this exercise. You'll have time to reflect later.
- Some people like to begin gluing immediately. Others like to place the items and then cut or re-tear them to fit in the spaces and relationships that emerge as the piece is created. If you're daring and it seems appropriate, burn the edges of some or all of the paper pieces. But whatever your preference of assembly, do it without considering why you're arranging things the way you are. Let openness guide you and don't judge yourself as you work. Most people will choose to arrange the paper items first without gluing and then arrange non-paper items on top, weaving them into the fabric of the piece as a final step. Then, after figuring out the spacing and how to incorporate the non-paper items, begin gluing. If you are working with some heavy items, it's usually best to secure them with a glue gun and then apply any paper items over them.
- As a final step, consider adding color by using acrylic paints or markers. Continue to work without much reflection on where God is drawing you in this prayer.
- After you complete the piece, sit back, take a deep breath, close your eyes, and take a few minutes to let go of the creative process. Don't be surprised if you find yourself tired or even exhausted. If you've jumped deeply into the places of your faith and culture and asked God to help

you learn a new language of prayer, you will have used an incredible amount of energy and emotion. But don't be surprised if you have lots of energy. You may have discovered a new place of strength within you.

- When you've rested and thanked God for the creative process, look at your creation. Sit with it and gaze into it for clues to where God is transforming the language of your prayer. Use the soul questions that follow to delve deeper into how God is transforming the language of your prayer.

- Give thanks for all the beauty you see, for the openness that you encounter and the discovery that you now enjoy. Analyze, but go slowly. You will have this piece as long as you choose to keep it and there'll be ample time to discover where you are called through it.

- Finally, put it in an inconspicuous place and let it become a part of your life, a continuing prayer.

Soul Questions

- What language from your tradition has trapped God and denied God's love and freedom to you?
- What language from society or from your vocation has kept God from being present with you?
- What language from your tradition has been helpful along the journey?
- What biblical passages do you most identify with and why? Are there other spiritual narratives, from the saints or from your own life, that are present in your collage?
- What do these stories say about how God is calling you or how God is liberating your prayer?
- How does the collage reveal a need to dig deeper into Scripture? What things amazed you about the biblical narratives you could recall or relate to during the exercise?
- How did the collage surprise you?
- What discoveries have you made about yourself and God?

Tools for the Journey

- What is your earliest memory of Scripture? Who told you the story? Why do you think it made such an impression on you?
- What is your favorite hymn? Look at its words. Are they comforting?

Have you ever really taken the time to study them and see what they mean to you?

- Write a kindergarten ditty to tell a story of Scripture. How does it feel to hear the story as a child? What things do you hear from the perspective of a child that you miss as an adult?
- Go to a library or bookstore and look at the pictures in a children's Bible. What do to the images say to you?

WINDOW THREE
Creating Holy Space

When they came to the place that God had shown him,
Abraham built an altar there and laid the wood in order. He
bound his son Isaac, and laid him on the altar, on top of the
wood. Then Abraham reached out his hand and took the knife
to kill his son. But the angel of the Lord called to him from
heaven, and said, "Abraham, Abraham!" And he said, "Here
I am." He said, "Do not lay your hand on the boy or do
anything to him . . . And Abraham looked up and saw a ram,
caught in a thicket by its horns . . . So Abraham called that
place "The Lord will provide."

Genesis 22:9–14

As a child, I was horrified by the story of Abraham and Isaac. How on earth could God ask Abraham to sacrifice his son? Why would a loving God even consider it? I didn't care that God provided another sacrifice and that Isaac was spared. The thought that God would ask Abraham to sacrifice his son was offensive and I remember telling my poor Sunday school teacher so. I'm not so sure she knew what to think about me.

But now I realize that Abraham building an altar and placing his son on it—and God sparing the child just in the nick of time—isn't really a story about the patriarch's faithfulness. The whole point of the story—indeed the whole theme of the Creator's passion for us throughout history—is that God is faithful. Whenever and wherever we find it within ourselves to build an altar and present our life and labor to God, the Holy One will bless it in faithfulness. Abraham was faithful to the divine's request, but it was the holy faithfulness that gave meaning to the story for the children of Israel. God made a promise to raise up a nation to set the people free and the Almighty would keep that word.

Unfortunately, we've made most altars untouchable. We've sequestered God into a space behind a rail and only those trained to walk lightly around the Divine are entitled to go near. Altars have become objects of adoration and piety, as if beautiful and inaccessible altars somehow had a connection to God's faithfulness. But the whole point of Abraham's altar before God was its accessibility; it was smack in the midst of life with all the challenges and frustrations our journey brings.

In the history of the Church, altars began just like that—honest expressions of vulnerability when the people gathered together as Christ's body. In the early Church, the people of God used a plain, simple table as their altar. Largely underground and persecuted, early Christians celebrated within their homes and their altars were everyday pieces of furniture. Plain bread, wine, cheese, and olives were placed on their tables, but through the communal sharing of God's words over those gifts, the ordinary became a window into the sacred, into the soul of God. Their tables became an extension of God's table.

Later, when Constantine became a Christian and Christianity became mainstream, the altar moved out of the home. Over time, as the Church became more and more institutionalized, the altar and all its trappings became specialized. Eventually, the altar was used only for the sacraments of the Church and became increasingly off limits—its connection to daily life was lost. By the time of the high Middle Ages, screens and rails separated the altar completely from the people of God. In most cases, they couldn't even see it.

During the Reformation of the sixteenth century all that changed. The altar was freed from screens and rails and made visible again. Once again, the altar represented the everyday lives of the people before God. In most Christian traditions today, the altar is accessible. High altars with chancel rails remain here and there, but even so, the altars of our churches are mostly free standing and unencumbered. Despite all the changes, most people think of the altar as something only for the church, and not for home or personal use. Average Christians haven't claimed an altar as an everyday item.

But an altar is a wonderful place to reflect on your life before God. It can be built anywhere that's meaningful to you, and you can fill it with any items that have spiritual significance in your life. My spiritual director has a beautiful room with chairs centered around a simple table, and water flowing from a small fountain. Stained glass is juxtaposed with contemporary expressions of mercy and two of God's delightful creatures, Yorkshire Terriers, sit at our feet while we open ourselves up to God's presence. But the most amazing thing about the room is its altar-ness. It's as if the entire room is an altar before and with God.

All over the room, in carefully selected places, my director has placed gifts given to her by friends and directees. On one side is a small rock from someone's sacred journey while on another is a book of poetry that expressed someone's soul on an important occasion. Sitting across the room is a picture of a family and in the middle of the table is a shell gathered, perhaps, on a beach walk that began lonely yet ended in hope.

Altars can also be built in places not normally considered sacred, at least not in the church sense. In the first studio where I worked, my mentor placed important images and objects throughout the creative space and encouraged me to do the same. In one area, she constructed a shelf that contained reminders of places she'd been and images of places she wanted to go. Later, just after my grandmother died, I created such a space in my own home. Just weeks after she died, I awoke in the middle of the night, horrified, feeling lonely, abandoned, and lost. It seemed as if I were losing my whole life, suffocating amidst memories I didn't understand. Over time, and by the grace of God, I came to realize that the memories made little sense because they were the memories of a seven-year-old. Events that weren't addressed then had found their way deep down within my soul, sealed away in darkness, and I had no real way to understand them or deal with them. When my grandmother died, she was the only other person who shared those memories with me, and so without her, I faced them alone. I had a choice: face them and let light come to the darkness or fall deeper within the abyss letting the darkness swallow me and my life.

After dealing with her death and discovering that many of my fears were those of a seven-year-old, it became increasingly important to find connections to that earlier time in my life and present them all to God, trusting that my Creator would be there. Slowly, over time I scavenged a baseball from the closet, my red plaid lunch box from the basement, and crayon drawings from a box my mother had hidden in the guest bedroom closet. I began to find pieces of my life that I could hold once again, asking how they were significant, who the boy was who had used or made them, and what they meant for me today.

These objects became important to finding the holy in my life. One by one, they started appearing on a shelf in my studio. Gradually, I added a candle to light when I was working in clay, rocks from my soul's homeland, Ireland, pictures of my family and other significant people, and events that could be captured by something tangible. From time to time, art found its way into the space as well. I'd add a recent sculpture or collage, for example, that reflected my journey. But most importantly, I found a way to express my spiritual life in the form of an honest and open altar before God. With Abraham, I reached deep within my life to present to God *all* of the person I was created to be, trusting that God would be faithful, loving, and embracing.

To this day, I continue to find ways to create altars all around me. Above my desk where I have written this book hangs a pop art crucifixion in oil. To the side is a picture of me with my children. In another place, hanging over files, is a small cross a mentor gave me many years ago. And from time to time, I place a stick or rock from my son's adventures in the yard into the mix. My desk at the church is no different. A paperweight from my daughter, a picture of my wife and me dancing, a small box from my best friend, and an icon from a beloved artist all surround me and keep me centered and honest about who I am and how faithful God is in the midst of my life.

Is your altar open before God? Is it hidden behind the screens of life? Is it just the altar of the church, some marble table far away, distant and impersonal? Or have you pushed through to see your own holy place before God? These are the questions for our prayer.

Prayer Three: Creating Your Altar to God

Time Required: Initial Set-up 1 hour

Opening Prayer

God, open my life to you that I might present all of who I am upon the altar that you give me. Amen.

Materials and Prayer Method

- Consider recent events and people in your life. Where are you with your job, your family, and your sense of God—whatever you are facing in life?

- Identify and collect objects that capture the essence of the feelings that you have about job, family, God, whatever is in your life right now. You might consider recent photographs, bulletins, or programs from events you've attended, or small mementos of places or people who are significant in your journey.

- Find a place to create your altar. It can be on a shelf or a table, or in any location that appeals to you. For some, an open area where others can see the altar will be problematic. If so, choose a more private spot where you are comfortable displaying the objects you create. Other people may choose to place their altar in an accessible place and even invite others to look at it. Whatever the case, make sure it is in an area that you will visit often. The whole purpose of assembling your altar is to deepen your spiritual journey. If you fail to participate in the space you create, you will fail to journey with it and through it with God.

- Honor the place you have chosen and mark it as sacred.
  - You can use a simple prayer, something as easy as "God, bless this place and my life in it." Or you might consider a more involved prayer, naming the concerns of your life before God and how those needs may be reflected in this space you are about to create.
  - You could acknowledge the divine's presence there already by simply thanking God for being in your holy space and in your life. Mark your gratitude with words, with silence, or with a breath prayer, by inhaling and exhaling while considering God's presence in your life. Some people enjoy burning incense or sprinkling the area with water—both ancient signs of blessing and holiness within the Christian tradition.
  - You might repeat the collage prayer from Window One as a way to discover where you are in relationship with God.
  - Consider reading the story of Abraham and Isaac in Genesis 22. Think about what it meant for Abraham to trust in God's faithfulness and reflect on your own experience of trust and faith. Or read a poem that you feel blesses the space.

– Please don't worry. There is no right way or wrong way to thank God for the holiness that is present in your life. The sky's the limit when it comes to expressing your gratitude toward God and asking for blessings upon your holy space.

• Construct your altar. Assemble pieces in whatever order you choose. You might drape a cloth over the area and arrange boxes or other elevated spaces under the cloth to make more objects visible and accessible to you.

• Add a candle to light when you are present with your living altar. You might even add incense, potpourri, fresh flowers, or herbs. If you do add a burning candle or incense, be sure to take the necessary fire precautions.

• Add to the area as the need arises. As you complete exercises in the following chapters, you might consider adding your creations to your holy space.

• Write out daily prayers or petitions and place them at the altar. Add other items as well. If a loved one is sick and you are praying for healing, put that person's picture on your altar. If you hold anger or resentment against someone, add a picture or name them by placing their written name there. If you're angry with God, make something that embodies that frustration. If you're celebrating an anniversary, birthday, or other significant event, praise God with the cards you receive or something that you make. Whatever is going on in your life, present it to God at the altar.

• As your prayers are answered, create offerings of thanksgiving and place them before God.
  – If you have written out petitions, write about how the prayer was answered.
  – Use pictures, objects, and other art forms to mark thanksgiving. If a loved one is healed, place her picture at the altar and surround it with confetti, flowers or other objects of celebration.

• Make room for prayers of praise and adoration. Tell God how you feel, how honored you are to be God's beloved, make an object or write a prayer that celebrates God's presence in your life. Hymns or song texts are useful ways to find words of praise as you pray.

• Consider adding a tape recorder or CD player to the area. If you're a musician, don't hold back! Take your guitar to the altar. Or if you've never played an instrument in your life, buy a tambourine or bell—anything that helps you celebrate or express yourself at the altar. After all, sometimes music speaks for us when we can't tap into our own creativity. Honor God, yourself, and your life with God in prayers of song.

• Invite friends over for a dedication of the space if that feels right. Ask your priest or minister to come for a house blessing and have a party afterwards.

Soul Questions

• What was it like to carve out a space within the home or office to honor God?
• What worries came to the surface?
• What emotions did you feel while working?
• What surprises came your way?
• How honest do you feel you're being with God?
• How does your altar make it easier for you to be present with God, listening and waiting for God's voice in your life?

Tools for the Journey

• Draw a picture of the very first altar you remember. If you can't remember the altar itself, draw a picture of the first thing that you remember as holy or God-like.
• Look around your house and yard. In addition to the altar you have created, what other holy spaces do you see? Consider adding that swing you've always wanted in the back yard or adding a simple fountain to your porch to carve out more holy space in your life.
• Go to a field of flowers or find a beautiful tree in your yard or a nearby park. Discover the holy in the petals or in the curves of the tree's leaves. If you can, take a couple of flowers or leaves and place them on your altar.
• Consider a retreat, setting a time apart in a safe place you believe is holy. While retreat centers and monastic communities make great places to re-connect with God, sometimes it's important to go where we feel led—the beach, mountains, or down by the river. Also, don't limit retreat to several days away. Sometimes a half-day in a city park can do wonders for the soul.

WINDOW FOUR
Praying Each Day

Pray in the Spirit at all times in every prayer and supplication.

Ephesians 6:18

Praying each day is a constant challenge. In the hectic pace of our lives, we often forget to try praying regularly. We spend far more than eight hours at work, run home to spend time with family, and exhausted, turn on the television to relieve ourselves of life's constant responsibilities. Even in moments of rest, most of us are multitasking—thinking about work or puzzling over problems and challenges at home. We're addicted to a lifestyle of constant activity and stimulation, so sitting down to a quiet time of listening for God is an almost alien activity.

So when we do get around to praying, we sound more like we're reciting a Christmas list than entering into relationship with God. We take our shopping-mall mentality to God and expect a warehouse portion of blessings in return. It's as if praying at God were just another item on our to-do list, instead of a foundational relationship to our identity with our world, our creator, and ourselves. But even in the midst of such empty prayers, we drift away from our petitions and fall back into our busy lives; our petitions before God become a mere reminder of what we have to do tomorrow or next week. "God bless Aunt Sue" becomes "And oh, I have a meeting at noon" or "Shoot, I forgot the paper towels at the store." Most of us can't be still and silent. We can't let our hearts sit and listen for the voice of God. Listening has become impossible as constant activity, and the noise it generates, is our refuge and strength. Turning to silence, and thus to God, has become insufferable.

And yet we know that God speaks in silence. Think of Moses. Think of Samuel. Think of Job. These pillars of the faith came to know the voice of God as one of screaming silence. They took the time to listen intently for the voice of God, knowing full well that God didn't speak in answers but most often in questions. God moved among them silently, quietly leading the way to things unseen, unheard, and unknown. They became charter characters of the faith because they understood how to be still, sit, listen, and discern the path and journey that God blessed.

Mandalas provided that key to daily prayer for me. Mandalas are an ancient form of soul-searching. Used mostly in the Eastern religions of Hinduism and Buddhism, they are circular representations of the soul's journey in this world. Traditionally, they were created during meditation and functioned as the metaphor for the soul's discovery while contemplating the meaning of life in the present moment. Over time, a complex discipline evolved around these ancient prayer tools. Quadrants were defined as corresponding to certain emotions or responses to events in life. Colors were assigned significance, as were outer bands and other forms of expression. Words were prohibited in early mandalas, but later creators included words written in Sanskrit.

Carl Jung, the great psychiatrist and researcher who was concerned with the connection between the mind and soul, found these circle prayers foundational to the spiritual life. He felt that they were an external portrayal of the inner life, one that could be grasped by others. The art of the mandala provided a pathway to the melodies of life—music that might be composed of different notes and rhythms but with a base melody in which we all find a common thread. Because of Jung's writings, especially on how the mandala related to dreams and the subconscious mind, these artistic prayers gained universal exposure. Over time they've been transformed into an ecumenical form of prayer shared among the religions of the East and West. No longer limited to meditative traditions of Buddhism and Hinduism, they became a new kind of icon for many in the Christian tradition and provided a window to the soul of the believer.

Prayer Four: Mandalas

Time Required: 30 minutes or less

Materials

- Paper. An unlined journal or sketchbook is a perfect resource when beginning a discipline of daily mandala meditations. A loose-leaf notebook with unlined paper inserted also works well and is inexpensive.
- Colored pencils.
- Markers.
- Pastels.

Opening Prayer

Creator, help me see with your eyes that all the colors of your world might be mine. Amen.

Prayer Method

Find a quiet place in your home or in a location where you have the time and space to meditate. Pay special attention to comfort. Going outside might work sometimes if you select a protected, quiet spot with few distractions. City parks often make a great spot.

- Be sure to turn off all phones, radios, televisions, and any other devices that would interrupt you.
- Take several minutes to begin listening. Some of us will be drawn into the creative process immediately and will want to begin working as soon as thoughts and images come. Others will take considerably more time before the process unfolds. Either way, try to take at least twenty minutes to listen for God before you begin.
- From time to time, you might consider using the practice of *lectio divina* during your twenty minutes of listening. The process of lectio divina, or divine reading, is simple. Select a passage from Scripture, a narrative that's been important to you, or some other writing that has been pivotal on your spiritual journey. If you're stuck, you could use a devotional book as a resource or make selections from the lectionary, a systematic method of reading the scriptures available in most book stores or even online. At first, select shorter passages that take about two to three minutes to read aloud. Once you get into lectio divina as a regular practice you can move on to longer passages. The process is pretty straightforward. Select your passage and then read it aloud. While reading, listen for the word or phrase that calls to you. If you want, repeat the reading two or three times, each time noticing the

words or phrases that grab your attention. If you can let go of all the busy-ness in your life and listen intently for the word or phrase, the Holy Spirit will guide you and the word you need will be provided. Once you have heard the word or phrase, repeat it over and over as your mantra during the twenty minutes of silence. Let the word become your prayer.

- After meditating on the word or phrase, or, if you're not using lectio divina, after just sitting in silence listening, begin working on the mandala.
- Spread all the pencils, pastels, markers, and other items on your workspace. You'll want to be able to work with all the colors as they come to you. Quick access is important.
- Draw a circle that will form the boundary of your mandala. Consider adding outer bands or wheels to the circle, areas in which to put words, phrases, or drawings. You'll want to cover most of the page with the circle and bands.
- Begin working inside the circle. You're not planning a drawing but allowing the creative energy kindled by the meditation or lectio divina to guide you. Draw and doodle whatever images come to mind. For some of us, abstract drawings will be our main focus. For others, more realistic images may come.
- Resist the urge to plan; just let it come to you. Work with fluid hand movements and remember that you can come back to the drawing later if you want to refine the work.
- Work quickly without considering your work intellectually. When we slow down and start reflecting, we tend to become critical. We stop listening or paying attention to God through our prayer, and technique and perfectionism creep in. But if we work spontaneously, the subconscious within expresses itself and the soul's interaction with God is open. The interior life we fail to see becomes visible through the creative process.
- If you want to create more than one mandala, do so. Continue working for the whole period you've set aside. I often create four or five mandalas at a sitting.
- When finished, place the mandalas before you. Look for common themes and begin to reflect upon how the designs reflect the prayer of

your soul. How do they bear your soul more fully into the world?

• If you choose to keep your mandalas in a journal or binder, return to them from time to time. Consider the path they paint and how your life with God grows through them.

Soul Questions

• Why is it difficult to pray daily?
• How do the mandalas help you shed the busy life you lead? How do they help you stay focused in prayer?
• If you tried lectio divina, what was it like? Did the word or phrase change with subsequent readings or were they the same? What did the word or phrase mean to you at this point in your life?
• How was the meditative process reflected in your prayer mandala?
• What surprises did you encounter?
• What challenges did you face?
• How might the mandala open your heart to a new relationship with God?

Tools for the Journey

• What is your earliest memory of color?
• Go outside and notice the colors. Don't look at form but just the colors. What do you see? Pay special attention to different shades of the same color. How does light affect the colors? What do you notice as the light changes?
• What color do others say looks good on you? How do you like that color?
• Do a series of mandalas. Be sure to date them. How does color relate to your spiritual journey as you look back at them? Do certain colors correspond to certain feelings as you review the mandalas? Do these themes and relationships also correspond to your earliest memory of color, the color that looks good on you, or the colors you are drawn to in nature?
• If you don't have time to do a mandala each day, try this variation. Close your eyes. What color immediately comes to mind? Do you have any idea why? Try this over an extended period of days and write the color at the top of each day's journal entry. Review the entries from time to time and consider the same questions just listed for reflection on mandalas.

WINDOW FIVE
Surprised by Miracles

*Jumping up, he stood and began to walk, and he entered the
temple with them, walking and leaping and praising God . . .
and they recognized him as the one who used to sit and ask for
alms at the Beautiful Gate of the temple; and they were filled
with wonder and amazement at what had happened to him.*

Acts 3:8–10

Not long ago, my wife and I went to the mountains to spend the weekend
in a friend's cabin. We traveled in the midst of winter and were looking forward to the cabin, a roaring fire, good food, wine, gently falling snow, and
the quiet of each other's company.

As we made our way, the cell phone rang. Our hosts were calling to
say that they'd heard there was a lot of snow on the ground and that more
was coming, promising to make the drive difficult. We were in our station
wagon—hardly an all terrain vehicle, but good at most situations—so I
wasn't afraid. We could handle it. I reassured our hosts, but they insisted
that we might not make it up to the cabin. So, we listened to instructions
about where to park, how to walk up the mountain to the house, retrieve
the four-wheeler in the basement, drive back down to our luggage, and
then return to the cabin quickly—a twenty-minute ordeal. It sounded simple, even adventurous, and we drove on, excited about the trek before us.

When we arrived, I went into the real estate office at the base of the
mountain, explained our plans, and asked if we could park there. No
problem, they answered. Graciously, a man offered to take us up in his
four-wheel drive vehicle. Wonderful, we thought! That would make things

so much easier. Thankful, we loaded all into a Subaru and headed up the mountain.

And a mountain it was. About a half-mile up, things started to look really rough. The road had washed away, and large gullies stood where others had traveled and where melting snow had formed mini canyons. Things became more treacherous the farther we went. We asked how far the cabin was, especially since we were traveling in what seemed a vertical line. "Oh, a mile or two," came the response. My wife just looked at me, the fear in her eyes meeting the anxiety in my own.

But we kept going, slipping and sliding the whole way. As we faced a large bank to the right and a bluff to the left, I thought we might meet our maker. But that was nothing compared to The Hill. It stood before us, a huge vertical climb covered in snow. And our driver, seemingly undaunted by it, merely pressed the pedal to the floor, "gunning it," he said. We were shot out of a cannon, traveling far too fast on the snow and ice, as if we'd been catapulted into an artic roller coaster. The van slipped, rolled sideways, backward, any direction at all, but somehow we kept going forward, ever moving toward the top. Several times my wife gripped my hand so tightly that I thought amputation was awaiting. And then, just as fast as we had started up, we stopped. We were stuck. We could go no farther.

"You'll have to walk the rest of the way," he said matter-of-factly. And so, on the side of a mountain, with about eight inches of snow freshly fallen on several layers of ice, we set out with our luggage, food—everything we'd brought. "I'll meet you here on Monday," our kind driver said with a smile, closing the back door of the van, jumping in, and sliding down the side of the mountain, tailpipe spewing smoke as we watched him disappear.

I looked at my wife. She looked at me. We were standing on the side of a mountain, clouds rolling in, temperature about fifteen degrees, and all our belongings for the long weekend scattered on the ground. After taking a moment to rest and gather ourselves for the walk to the house, we set out to the cabin and to the four-wheeler that would be our miracle worker and deliverer.

We walked about half a mile in the snow, up hills—they call them mountains where we live—and down the other side, till we saw the most picturesque cabin sitting on the side of the mountain. New energy claimed us and we made our way, a spring in our step. We walked to the house and it was wonderful—a grand, simple, colorful, soothing, expressive, grace-filled kind of place. The kind of house that feels like coming home, as if, as the Celts believed, a part of your soul had already been there and you were encountering more of yourself in just finding your way to it.

We went to the basement, found the four-wheeler, started it, and saw the impossible: a flat tire. And not just any flat tire; it was a FLAT tire. Neither one of us could find a pump. We looked for a compressor, something, anything, but there was nothing. Reality began to sink in. We would have to make three or four trips to the cabin carrying the suitcases, coolers, and bags filled with everything we'd brought for the weekend. So much for starting the relaxing weekend right away.

We began to look around for a wagon or cart and found a recycling bin on wheels. We walked the half-mile back to our belongings and loaded as much as we could onto the cart. Of course, a cart in eight inches of new snow and ice doesn't help all that much, but it did help a little. It was way below freezing, but even so, I was sweating like crazy as we made our way back to the cabin with load number one. And then load number two. And then load number three. All in all, it took just over two hours to gather our belongings into the cabin. Somewhere during load number two I realized that in five days we'd be doing this again. Not a great thought.

We got everything inside, built a fire, opened a bottle of wine, and tried to unwind. We were exhausted and more than a little sore. We were glad to be there, but it was hard to be thankful for the time away after the difficulty of getting there. And then the phone rang.

It was the owners, our friends, calling to check on us. "Well, we finally made it," I said, not saying anything about the ordeal we'd been through. "Did you use the four-wheeler?" he asked. I explained the flat tire. "Oh, you should use the compressor." "What compressor?" I replied while thinking, "No way, absolutely no way." Our host explained that the compressor was under a tarp in the garage. What we needed had been there all along; we just hadn't seen it. Deliverance had been right beside us, but in our own blindness we didn't know it.

I remember hanging up the phone and realizing we had a choice: We could be sad, angry, or even hysterical. Or we could laugh.

It was at that point I saw the *milagros*. All over the house were small medals from Central America. Our hosts, who had a business there, had collected lots of these wonderful little prayers. "Milagros," the Spanish word for miracles, are the outward symbols of a prayer. In Central America and some parts of the Mediterranean, people express their innermost petitions by placing these small medals all over the place. Made of silver, aluminum or other inexpensive metals, they adorn crosses, statutes, doors, windows, frames, and other objects within a parish, house or village. You even find them along roadways on posts, signs, and trees.

For the person praying with them, they express both the prayer offered and the miracle sought. If a small child needs healing, a medal of a boy or girl might be nailed to a wooden cross. If a pet is missing, a dog or cat medal might be pinned on a statue of Saint Francis.

But a person's prayer is not offered in isolation. Milagros are placed together. Hundreds of the medals are pinned on saints, crosses, and altars. The prayer for a pet is next to a prayer for a dying child. The parent's hope for healing is paired with a toddler's hope for a new tricycle. No prayer is too small or too grand for God. None is elevated above the other.

It was in seeing all the milagros in our hosts' home that we realized that we had been blessed. The icy, snowy road had actually been a road to a miracle. We just didn't know it at the time. But seeing our experience in the context of all those medals, realizing we shared our life and labor with the whole hosts of God's people, made all the difference.

Prayer Five: Milagros and Intercessory Prayer

Time Required: 1 hour

Opening Prayer

God help me to see the miracle of my life and how you sustain me each day with your abundant grace and love. Amen.

Materials

- A frame, holy box, or object. Try a small shadow box or other item that can hold objects of various sizes. At a recent rummage sale, I purchased a 1940s homemade dollhouse for less than a dollar. About one foot high and three inches deep, it has two rooms with an open roof at the top. It makes a perfect house for my milagros. Wood cutouts of crosses, simple cigar or shoeboxes, or other objects all make excellent frames or containers for applying the milagros.

- Collect medals or charms that reflect your prayer life. If you want a really traditional-looking milagros application, look for the medals in a local crafts store or inquire at a local *tienda*—a Central American grocer. Many online auction sites have them, as well as some suppliers of silver jewelry from Central America. Sometimes you can find a dozen or more of the milagros medals for less than a dollar. But don't limit yourself to the traditional medals. You can use cutouts from magazines, Christmas cards, or other mixed media as medals. By using a variety of cutout milagros you can produce an impressive but inexpensive collage.
- For mounting ideas, visit a scrap-booking store. Scrapbook supplies and techniques can really make paper objects come alive. You can raise some objects for a three-dimensional effect, surround them with paper frames and other accents, or even cut images into mosaics for an interesting application.
- Consider mixing traditional milagros with other objects. Combine objects such as Mexican medals, cutouts, small keepsakes, natural objects, and other items that express your thanksgiving, petition, intercession, or praise in prayer.

Prayer Method

- Prepare the workspace. Find a quiet spot to work and give yourself plenty of room.
- Set up the area with all the materials so you won't be interrupted during the prayer. Take all the objects you've selected, as well as the piece you're using for mounting.
- When mounting, select the method that best suits the items you've selected. Collage will work best with rubber cement. Traditional milagros and small objects respond best to a glue gun. Heavier objects might require an epoxy with an extended drying time. If you want to remove some or all of the objects so you can hold them during subsequent meditations with the milagros, consider using Velcro. Sometimes you can line a whole framework with the "smooth" side of the Velcro, creating a soft background for the application of your milagros. It's like creating your own felt board, and it functions as a kind of

prayer board for you. You can also use the stick-on variety of Velcro available in most craft stores. With the stick-on tape, affix one side to the milagro and the other to the object you're mounting it on. Cut the tape small enough that you don't see it. The background of the mounting object will show through beautifully.

- When you've gathered all the supplies and determined your mounting method, begin your prayer. Arrange the items on the box, frame, or other item you have selected paying attention to each of the objects you have selected and how they relate to each other. When you're ready, begin mounting them with the glue or method chosen.
- After the application has dried, place the milagros into your holy space created in Window Three.
- Add additional prayers over time. When one framework is full, begin another.

Soul Questions

- What milagros did you identify in your own life? On behalf of others?
- If you included prayers for others, what was it like to see your prayer next to a petition or intercession for another?
- Do you think of your prayers as miracles, or is this a new experience for you? What does it feel like to identify the petition or thanksgiving as a miracle?
- How can you make milagros a part of your everyday life?
- Could focusing on miracles transform our prayers from seeking results into living faithfully?

Tools for the Journey

- Go looking for miracles with a child. Toddlers are really great; their responses are uninhibited. Ask them to show you all the neat things they see in a park or at the zoo. Try to see the world as they see and describe it.
- Write a story about a miracle in someone's life. Healing, recovery, change in attitude are all possibilities.
- Make a list of the challenges you face in your life—financial, emotional, physical, spiritual. What miracles do you desire in each area? Write prayers for each one or use the milagros exercise to petition God for these miracles.

44

WINDOW SIX
Living in the Moment

So don't worry about tomorrow, for tomorrow will bring its
own cares. Today's cares are enough for today.
Matthew 6:34 (Author's translation)

One of the hardest windows to open is that of living in the moment. But the key to opening this window is realizing that each moment is a gift to be treasured for what it is, in and of itself. When the moment is treasured, deep experience becomes possible, and the soul's connection to the creator and the created is uncovered. Then, and only then, do we see Christ in a child laughing, hear God in a loved one's voice, or taste God in the assurance of the bread we share. As the simplicity of the moment is embraced, the miracle of grace emerges no matter where we are, what we're doing, or how we feel.

Cancer and substance-abuse survivors have taught me this difficult lesson. I am repeatedly amazed to be around cancer patients who laugh at their disease and alcoholics who joke about the dark days of their addiction. The cancer patient, enduring the pain, the dehumanizing treatment, and the fear of death reacts with thanksgiving for the opportunity to see life in a new light. The alcoholic tells me about his gratitude for the recovery from a disease that tries to control each passing day. These survivors have seen the miracle of life itself and, having seen it, become more alive than ever. They've embraced living in the moment as the pathway to wholeness in their lives.

These children of God teach us the importance of living one day at a time. They tell stories of telling God off, unlearning prayer, and pushing through chaos to the other side—a place where they rest in the arms of Christ and bask in grace. They show us that it's possible to uncover a place of total openness before God. Sometimes, they push through to a place that empowers them to let go so that God can hold them as God's own. At other times they find a place of compassionate playfulness, rolling along the floor with God, laughing in spite of all that life can bring.

I recall one moving example of pushing through to rest in the arms of God. A father faced the unbelievable diagnosis of cancer in his two-year-old daughter. He walked up and down the street outside the hospital for hours; he was angry, frustrated, worried, and just plain fed up. He had no idea what to do. There were no more doctors to seek, no more tests to run, no more of the usual prayers to be offered. He felt paralyzed, powerless, and impotent in the face of it all. And then, in a state of desperation, without really thinking about it, he looked up to heaven and shook his fist at God. He told God how he really felt. He wasn't even sure how long he ranted. But when he finished, he felt liberated and alive. From that moment on, no matter what happened, he knew he'd pushed through—he'd been open, transparent, real with God. And in that space, he rested in God's arms of mercy.

Another time a boy, dying of cancer, yelled at me, insisting that I get out of his room, insisting that the God I loved was useless to him. Minutes later, he sobbed uncontrollably and told God off as I held him in my arms. The next day, his whole disposition had changed and he never looked back. He'd pushed through his anger and frustration, through his disease, to find a compassionate God rolling along the floor with him, laughing in spite of it all. He faced his disease, and in God's own way, God healed this boy as they laughed together to the last gasp for air.

When we open ourselves to the moment—like the man and the boy I've described—and allow our whole being to be present to God, we encounter who we were created to be. Opening up space to be a real human being, the creature before God, the one called to be open and vulnerable, is what living in the moment is all about. We peel away the layers of our world that enslave us and return to the place where the soul encounters God. While we sometimes start with pain and suffering, with all the rough places of our experience, it's our voice crying in the wilderness that ultimately collides with the freedom and grace that God offers in the Son. For when we speak clearly in the moment and offer our lives up to God, we offer them to the cross. It is in giving all the pain and sorrow, all the sin and disappointment over to the care of God, that we discover the passion of God for us. When we risk standing outside the hospital yelling at God or telling God that we don't want to die of cancer, we turn the moments of our lives into moments of grace. We give ourselves back to God and liberation becomes possible.

Prayer Six: Word Collage II

Time Required: 1 hour

Opening Prayer

Help me to be honest with you God that in giving my whole self to you, I might find rest and renewal. Amen.

This method is similar to that used in the first prayer exercise but here it's more directed. Instead of just asking what interferes with your relationship with God, look intently at the moment before you. It's a more intentional exercise and one that challenges you to see your place with God—are you resting in arms of grace or rolling along the floor with God in laughter?

Materials

- White or colored poster board, construction paper, or a sheet of heavy card stock.
- Markers or colored pencils.

Prayer Method

- Arrange the paper and markers on a table in front of you. Reserve two bold markers for later in the prayer.
- Sit in a comfortable chair. Take a deep cleansing breath, breathing all the way in and then forcefully pushing all the air out. Repeat this breath three times.
- As your breathing returns to normal, begin to clear your mind. As we've done before, visualize placing any interruptions to the side, literally imagining a sticky note with the interruption on it if that helps.
- When you've quieted your mind, begin to meditate on the question, "What prevents me from living in the moment? Why do I resist resting in God's arms when I'm tired or sad, or laughing with God when I'm joyous?"

- In the first word collage, we wrote words and phrases to respond to the question. You're welcome to do that here as well, but if you can, also doodle answers to the question. Let the marker or pencil find its own way to express the answer through shapes, expressions of color, drawings, scribbles, and other expressions. For some, realistic doodling is possible and many pictures will be possible. You might draw a picture of where you are with God in this space and time. Others will construct more abstract or symbolic drawings using traditional forms or creative ones created during the prayer.

- If you struggle with sketches, try line contour drawings. Instead of focusing on the details of something you wish to draw, try to find the simplest way to express the idea, the way that uses the least amount of drawing. Essentially, you're attempting to capture just enough of the item for the imagination to know and thus fill in the rest. If you use this method, practice when you have a chance. Just sit in your room and find forms to quickly sketch, using as few lines as possible and working very quickly.

- When the doodling ends, take a moment to survey your work. Don't be critical; just ponder your creation. See what it is saying.

- After reflecting for twenty minutes or so, take one of the bold markers you reserved. Begin to draw and doodle answers that respond to a new question: "Why does God want me to trust in this moment?"

- Work quickly and continue as long as thoughts come to you. You can respond adjacent to each thing you've written or drawn, or you can respond thematically to the whole.

- When your response to the second question ends, take several minutes to reflect on your responses.

- Now, take the other bold marker you reserved and begin, haphazardly, to write words or phrases of things that might help you live in the moment with God. Here, I usually identify concrete steps I can take to slow down and push through to the other side, just like the father in the story or the teenager with cancer. In other words, how do I take steps toward falling into God's arms? How do I laugh with God?

- Continue to work as long as you can identify concrete steps you could take to live in the moment.

- When you've exhausted all the possibilities, live with the prayer. Allow the soul questions to guide your way.

Soul Questions

- What themes can you identify that prevent you from living in the moment? Which ones surprise you?
- What issues did you discover when you considered why God wanted you to live in the moment?
- Why is trusting God in the moment so difficult? What events in your life surfaced as you pondered God's desire for you? Have there been times when trusting God has been difficult for you?
- What concrete steps did you identify to help you live in the moment with God? Which ones can you use immediately? Which ones need more time? Consider establishing priorities among the steps and finding a way to mark your progress.

Tools for the Journey

- List three dreams you have given up on. How might living in the moment help you realize them?
- What is the silliest thing you've ever done? Try to recapture the moment by imagining it or writing about it. Why were you so free? What keeps you from being that way more often?
- Unlist your life! Write down all the things you want to do in the day. Leave a line between each task. Then, cut the list into separate strips. Concentrate on each item one at a time and give yourself only to that task. How does this help you live in the moment?
- Take off your watch one day and live without time. What is it like to take yourself off a schedule? Did you discover that you were able to accomplish more?

WINDOW SEVEN
Reconciling the Internal and External

All the paths of the Lord are steadfast love and faithfulness.

Psalm 25:10

Not long ago I was horrified when a man walked into my office weeping. I had no idea what had happened to him. As he sat with me, he began to tell me the story of a loved one who had died a couple of years earlier. His uncle, a boyhood hero and confidante, had been diagnosed with pancreatic cancer. At the time the doctors discovered the disease, they said there was nothing they could do. It was so advanced and spreading so rapidly that the doctors expected his uncle would only live six to eight weeks from the day they found it.

This man told me one of the most horrific stories I had ever heard, not about the cancer of his uncle, but the cancerous "faith" of someone who called himself a friend. This friend had told the man he needed to pray for the uncle's healing—not a bad suggestion. But weeks later, when his uncle died, the friend came back to him and declared, "Your uncle wouldn't have died if you were really a Christian. Your prayers weren't answered because God couldn't hear you. God gave you this opportunity to know salvation, to be saved, and you wasted it. If you had just believed, your uncle wouldn't have died. He would have lived." This fellow continued to pressure the man until a few days later, he led him through a prayer of salvation, asking God to forgive him for not answering the call earlier and for killing his uncle by not believing.

I wept. God's grace, freedom, and love had been reduced to some kind of thing, an object, a formula. The friend, honestly thinking he was introducing salvation, was taking this man down a road of guilt and frustration. The nephew was not only overcome with the grief of his uncle's death, the faith he was offered only increased his suffering. It played upon the internal doubts so many of us share—not feeling worthy, not good enough, not being the person God created us to be. Coupled with the external evidence of something going wrong, his doubt increased and his pain multiplied. Throughout our history, Christians have tied illness to not being right with God. All of us have heard it: "If he'd only believed more . . ." or "If they'd only trusted in God . . ." then x, y, z—the terrible thing—wouldn't have happened. And for some reason, we believe it. Sure, there are such themes in the Old Testament; we've all heard that the sins of the ancestors visit the generations that follow. But Scripture as a whole is more concerned with God's faithfulness to us, God overcoming disease and death, despair and depression, providing light that will not be overcome. Isn't it time for us to stop letting others steam roll those in pain by abusing them with a God of guilt, fear, and hatred? Isn't it time for our prayer life to reconcile all those inner doubts with the external evidence that often seems at odds with faithfulness? Isn't it time to admit that external realities are not evidence of a disinterested far-off God but the miracle of a God who suffers with us—a God willing to be one of us and suffer on the cross?

Prayer as art liberates us from fear and guilt because it seeks mystery, not certainty. The religion of fear and guilt hems us in. It makes us dishonest with one another and with God. When faced with hardship, we seek a happy face as evidence of good faith; if we can look happy, or even make ourselves feel happy, the pain might go away or at a minimum, the evidence of the internal doubt might be hidden from others. We put on and thus put up with the internal self-doubt that naturally flows from such a system. But when we embrace mystery in our lives, cancer, substance abuse, disease, depression, war, or other difficulties become opportunities to seize God's faithfulness to us instead of self-doubt. When we expose our fears openly and introduce them to the community of faith, we claim the possibility of resurrection for all the crosses of life. As such, moments of difficulty become opportunities to step beyond where we are into the unknown of God's faithfulness. God as mystery, revealed in sighs too deep for words, reconciles the conflict between internal doubt and external evidence. We stop seeking equilibrium and encounter a place of creative innovation with our God—a place where the soul finds its way home to the empty tomb of light.

Prayer Seven: Self-Portrait

Time Required: 1–2 hours

Opening Prayer

God, let me see myself as I really am—as your beloved child redeemed by your love and filled with your grace and mercy. Amen.

We now turn to the most revealing expression in the artist's portfolio: the self-portrait. Think of the masters' self-portraits through the ages. Van Gogh's reveals a man of profound introspection, Rembrandt's a person of piercing concentration and confidence. Each was able to identify the core of who they were on the canvas using very different styles and techniques. The same is true for all great self-portraits. Some artists paint realistic, almost photographic portraits, while others use abstraction. But the key is looking deep within, finding the core of the self, whatever it is. While likeness is important, finding and expressing something that conveys more than likeness, something that conveys the whole person, that's the key.

Materials

- A camera.
- For traditional photography, you'll need film, preferably black and white. Color film will also work but in many cases we capture more of ourselves with black and white. The lack of color leaves room for the imagination by emphasizing contrasts of light and dark. With a digital camera, you can choose to print your photographs in black and white, sepia tone, or color.
- Lots of old photographs of yourself. Be sure to include photos from childhood and youth as well as from your adult years.
- An inexpensive scrapbook.
- Two-sided tape, corner tabs, or rubber cement for mounting.

Prayer Method

- Take pictures! Have a trusted loved one snap pictures of you over a series of weeks. Give this person the camera to take snapshots any time you're doing something that captures who you are. Don't be bashful! Be yourself.

- Don't pose for pictures. Let the pictures happen. If your friend sees you being you, trust that the picture will capture the moment. In posed pictures, we most often smile, put on the public face we were taught as children, and cease to be ourselves. That's why so many studio portraits fail to capture the whole of us—they look like us but more than likely don't feel like us.

- Go through old pictures of yourself. Grab the ones that capture something of who you were at various stages in life. If life was joyous during college, look for a picture that captures those years. When you went through loss or sadness, look for that emotion in snapshots. You might be surprised by what you find.

- After you've collected lots of photos, set aside a time to look through and reflect on them. Set aside photographs that touch you, whether you like the picture or not. Let each photo speak for itself, and don't get caught up in whether your hair is neat or there's a funny expression on your face. Put aside the ones that capture you—all of you.

- Start arranging the photos into groups for mounting. You could organize them haphazardly, chronologically, or thematically, it's really up to you. But choose a format that will allow you to express who you are and that will capture major events and times in your life.

- Begin to arrange the photographs in your scrapbook. You might put one photo on a page if it figures prominently in your life. Other times will be best expressed with several photos or even a collage. Be sure to leave the page opposite each set of pictures blank.

- After mounting all the pictures, cut a sheet of paper that will fit opposite each page of the mounted photos. Use lined or unlined paper. Wait to mount the paper until you've finished the process.

- Meditate on each photograph or group of pictures mounted on a page. Using the paper you've selected, write a response to it. Use the soul questions to guide your process. As you write, don't limit yourself to prose. Write poetry, any words that come to mind in stream-of-consciousness, or even draw or doodle.

- Paste the reflections opposite the corresponding picture.

- When you've finished the process, live with the scrapbook for a while. Reflect on what you saw in yourself and what God sees in you.

Soul Questions for Writing the Reflections

- Why did you select this particular picture?
- What does the picture say about you to others? What does it say to you? Does the picture capture what you were feeling at the time?
- If others are in the picture, how are you relating to them? How are they relating to you?
- Does the picture reveal something that few people know about you?
- If you could change the picture, what would you do to it?

Soul Questions for Reflection on the Scrapbook

- How do the pictures capture your spirit? What evidence do you see of self-doubt?
- Are there particular times when the photos reveal more of you than at others? Are there any differences between good and bad times?
- What themes do you see?
- How does God react to this book? What would God see in each section?
- What do you discover about yourself in this book that you did not know before?
- Is anything missing from the photographs?
- How would the book differ if God had been taking the pictures?

Tools for the Journey

- Write a letter to yourself as if you were six years old. What would you say? What would you share? What would disappoint you about your present life? What would excite you?
- Write a letter to yourself twenty years from now. What challenges would you include? What dreams would you share? What hopes and aspirations?
- Go to a museum and look at the portraits. What do you see? What does the painting say about the *person*? Don't just consider how they look physically. What does the portrait say about the person spiritually?
- Check out a book of cartoons. What truths do they capture that a more "realistic" drawing might miss?

WINDOW EIGHT
Seeking Forgiveness

*The seraph touched my mouth with it and said: "Now that
this has touched your lips, your guilt has departed and your
sin is blotted out." Then I heard the voice of the Lord saying,
"Whom shall I send, and who will go for us?" And I said,
"Here am I; send me!"*

Isaiah 6:7–8

I remember well the first time I prepared for a confession. I was anxious and
had no idea what to do. I had grown up a Southern Protestant, and needless
to say, confession wasn't a part of our faith—people in my circle still
thought of it as Catholic and strictly taboo. We had the general confession
we said on Sunday, but private confession—just me and a priest—was a
totally different thing, and different wasn't better.

I headed off to seminary having never experienced personal confession
one-on-one with a minister. But my bishop, an Anglo-Catholic to the core,
replied to one of my early letters by remarking that I hadn't mentioned my
last confession when writing to him. He made it clear: confession was an
expectation. If I expected to be ordained as an Episcopal priest, confession
had to become a part of my spiritual discipline.

But my fear of it was too great, and so despite my bishop's letter, I didn't
go. It was just too strange and foreign. Then a second letter came.
"Michael, you did not mention confession in your report to me. GO! And
write me immediately to confirm. Faithfully, Your Bishop." Second time.
Second strike. One more and I'd be out. This time I had no choice; I had
to go.

So I found a faculty member I trusted. I went to him one afternoon and after talking about the weather and related topics for half an hour, I finally asked if he'd hear my confession sometime soon. "Sure," he said without batting an eye, "How about next Wednesday afternoon?" With all the horror and dread staring me in the face, there was no way out, no more delay, no way to put it off. We had an appointment. I was going to face this head on.

From there, I returned home, took out a piece of paper, and began writing. In many ways, it was an inventory of my life. At first, it was mostly generalities. Not loving God, lying, being rude to others, and things like that took up a whole page or so. But then the list became more specific. I remembered particular people I'd hurt and the exact things I'd done. Some of them were recent. Some were old. Some were even from my childhood—like the time I sent a friend to the hospital for stitches after a fight over a toy! I wrote down every little infraction I could think of. I remember congratulating myself about how good I was becoming at this confession thing. At the time, I wasn't wise enough to add my pride to my lengthy list of sins.

And so, with confession service in hand and list of sins ready to go, I went to the chapel the next week. I sat down and at the time appointed, the confessor walked in, sat beside me, purple stole and all. I began. "Bless me, for I have sinned." He responded, praying for the Lord to be in my heart and on my lips, that I might truly and humbly confess my sins. I took out my list. I read it. One after another, I confessed things that I'd done. Things I'd left undone. Things I should've done. And he sat there.

When I finished my list, I asked for counsel, direction, and absolution. And he sat there. With his wise eyes and a discerning heart staring at me, we just sat there in silence.

And then finally, be broke in with a surprise. "You have brought many things seeking God's forgiveness. Rightfully so. God has already heard you and forgiven you. But you have also brought too much —things that are not yours to bring, at least not as you have brought them. Why are all of those sins?" he asked, looking straight at me. "It seems that several of the things you list are not sins at all. You've commingled your grief over the sins of others with your own. They've got to be separated if you're going to find a pathway to wholeness. Asking forgiveness for sins that are not your own is not generous. It's dangerous," he concluded.

We finished the service, he granted absolution or forgiveness for my sins, and I went home. But the harder work began. He had challenged me to take a few weeks to figure out exactly what God had forgiven. He had told me to "figure out what was yours to bring. Then, come back. We'll go deeper." The act that I'd feared had opened a new part of the journey. Not only did I have a sense of the freedom that comes from hearing "You are forgiven—you are my child—welcome home," my soul had also been liberated from the sins of others. Like so many of us, I had held on tight to the hurts and pains of our life as human beings. But in holding so tightly, my grief and sadness had been mixed side by side with my sin. By seeing the distinction, I had experienced liberation. It took lots of work, but over time I was able to distinguish my feelings from my sins—not a small task in my experience.

The practice of confession opens a window to the soul by ritualizing the need for transparency with God. It begs us to be the creatures God created us to be, and to stop trying to be God. More than anything, confession calls us as individuals and as a corporate people to enter into that sphere of vulnerability where God stares deep within us and calls us his beloved children. It is the place where we hear again and again, "I love you. I cherish you. You are the terrific thing in my life."

Prayer Eight: Mixed-Media Self-Portrait

Time Required: 1 hour

Opening Prayer

God, you already know me and love me for who I am. Help me to believe in my belovedness before you. Amen.

In the last chapters we began the trek toward living without self-doubt, seeing ourselves as God sees us, and journeying into the mystery of God. Here, we build upon those exercises by using another form of self-portrait as a journey into forgiveness or confession. Diving into the honesty that confession creates allows a deeper sense of our belovedness to emerge. Seeking forgiveness becomes a window to love, freedom, and mercy in our lives. It's as if we push through, finally trust God enough to admit our faults, and then find ourselves resting in God's arms of faithfulness and mercy.

A self-portrait exercise makes clear how we have failed to trust God. We look at ourselves, literally, and find there all the trash with which we've filled our lives. We can identify where there's room to hear God say, "You are my beloved son, you are my beloved daughter," and from that place of accept-ance , we yell "Here I am" and we start living. We discover our true identity in Christ as we confess our faults with one who bore our faults, the one who already knows us as we are. An appendix is included for those who want to build on this exercise and explore personal confession with a minister or priest.

Materials

- Identify a picture you believe captures your soul. You might use one that came from Prayer Seven, or another portrait that you find partic-ularly insightful. If possible, select a photo of your whole body, not just a head-and-shoulders snapshot.
- Take the photograph to a print shop and have it blown up. An 11 x 14 or larger print will work best for this exercise. You can use a color or black and white copy, although I prefer the black and white for this prayer. It's not only less expensive to copy, the black and white con-trasts seem to fit the theme and practice better than color.
- Various markers, colored pencils, and other writing tools. If you can, also locate a gold, silver, or other metallic marker.
- Consider other items such as embossing wax, found at most craft supply stores in the stationery section, to create textured writing.
- Some cutouts of words for use as a collage application may also be used. The method outlined will help you identify appropriate words.

Prayer Method

- Prepare the area where you will work by assembling all the items you will need. Just as with the other exercises, take the necessary steps to make sure you'll have protected time free from interruption.
- Begin by thanking God for the time you have been given to consider who you are and how you have sinned against God and creation.
- Enter into a time of personal reflection. Meditate on the question "How have I sinned against God?"
- When thoughts of your sins begin to come to you, select a color and use it to answer the question by writing words or phrases on top of

your portrait. Use only that color for the question and reserve the metal-colored marker for later in the exercise.

• Consider whether the words or phrases that describe your sin belong in a particular place on the portrait. Is the sin present in your mind, your gut, or your heart?

• Don't worry about writing a story. Usually a single word or phrase will be sufficient.

• When you've exhausted that question, meditate on the question "How have I sinned against myself as God's beloved?" Repeat the process of answering by selecting another color marker, still reserving the metal-colored one, and putting down your thoughts and insights using that single color.

• Then, move on to the third question using another basic color to write your response. "How have I sinned against my neighbor?"

• If you like, you can also use cutouts or images when you answer the three questions. Magazine or newspaper headlines work also, as well as images from them. If you use this method, find a way to categorize the mixed media so that you know which question you are responding to. You could group your answers to each question or edge them with a color corresponding to each of the questions.

• When you've finished answering the three questions, return to the answers. Taking the metallic marker, or a bright color you haven't used, write what God's response would be to what you've written. God will always declare forgiveness, but could God also be asking you to go deeper? Are all the things you've written yours or are some of them the sins of others?

• Some may choose to take each of the three questions separately. You could use a different copy of your picture each time and use the exercise over three days if you choose.

• Another more difficult variation is to start without a picture and use cutouts to create the self-portrait. This method requires more creativity but anyone can do it. As with the first collage exercise in Window One, use a stream of consciousness approach to rip out pictures from old magazines while you reflect on the questions. Then, take the pictures and assemble them into a collage self-portrait. You can try to use shading or cutouts of facial features to create a facial form, or your self-portrait can be more abstract. Either way is fine. It's up to you!

- Upon completion, reflect on the whole process and notice the themes in your confession. Use the soul questions as a guide.
- If you decide to go to a confessor, use the self-portrait exercise to prepare for the process outlined in the appendix.

Soul Questions

- Were you surprised by the images that came to you when reflecting on the questions? What things did you remember that you thought you had forgotten?
- Are there connections between the sins you remembered from years ago and the sins you currently have in your life?
- What similarities did you note between your answers to the questions? What relationships do you see between your sins against God, your own self, and others?
- Did you write anything that's really not yours but someone else's?
- How is God asking you to go deeper? Is confession with another person something God is calling you to?
- Did the prayer help you see your sins visually? How about your forgiveness? What images of God's love did you see? How did God bless you through this process?

Tools for the Journey

- Make a list of all the parent figures in your life. How did they love you and shape your understanding of love? How did they support you and push you to believe in yourself? Have you ever thanked each of them for what they did for you? Consider writing them a letter.
- Think back to your earliest childhood memories. Did anyone tell you that you were bad? How do you still carry those comments? How can you let them go? Write a poem or short story about letting go. Imagine what would have happened in your life if you could have responded—now you can.
- Make a list of people that you need to forgive. How can you make amends? If they are still alive, find a way to do so. If they have died, write a letter to them asking forgiveness.

WINDOW NINE
Getting to the Cross

Then he said to them all, "If any want to become my followers, let them deny themselves and take up their cross daily and follow me. For those who want to save their life will lose it, and those who lose their life for my sake will save it.

Luke 9:23–24

Our journey has led us to the foot of the cross, God's level field for all people. This is really where we've been heading all along. We've opened our hearts honestly to God, found ways to let go of things that enslave our prayer lives, and discovered ways to be the people God created us to be. Now it's time to take the most significant steps of the journey home, as we walk with God toward the most significant windows to the soul—the cross and empty tomb. In this chapter, we go to the cross. For me, this was a difficult window to open.

I'd tried sculpting a crucifix many times before I finally created one. For so long I was stuck, stranded before the cross but not up close to it. I wanted to find myself within the story of the passion but I couldn't get there—it was just too vulnerable, too exposed, too abstract. Methods and techniques that had worked many times before had failed me. I couldn't reach that place of vulnerability with myself and with God.

But several years ago, I went to the studio after the Stations of the Cross service on Good Friday. There in the quietness and solitude of the studio, the story of the Stations opened up for me. I became intensely aware of Christ's suffering and began to see images of my own life nailed to the cross.

People, places, and events of pain and suffering were with Jesus on the cross. These images of Christ suffering with me came faster and faster as I took a piece of clay and meditated on what Christ had done for me. In sculpting that day, reflecting on all the things God took to the cross from my life, I found a place to let go and let God guide me to the level ground at the foot of the cross. The technical pains of the past slipped away as I entered a space where my thoughts, feelings, and creativity merged into one synchronistic dance. The passion of Christ, my life, and the present came together as I pushed and pulled the clay, slowly crafting a cross, a Jesus that I understood, that I could embrace.

Hours later, sweat pouring down my face, I realized that in sculpting that figure I had participated in the crucifixion of Christ. Staring back at me was a raw, unclothed Jesus, a Jesus without smooth skin, without a clean body, without a smile. This was the real Jesus, the mysterious one I'd been waiting for all along. This wasn't the black-and-white, I've-got-all-the-answers-in-a-tidy-little-book Jesus, a Jesus who would make me doubt and fear when life came my way. No, this was the Jesus who could be my savior, who could take my sins, who could transform my life because he participated in my life. This was the one who saw it as it was and endured it.

But the story didn't end there. I also placed Jesus in the tomb. I took a black plastic bag, a kind of body bag, and placed the whole crucifix inside. Practically, I was placing the clay there to dry, but spiritually, I was placing it there to die. I encased the whole thing in a makeshift wooden coffin and then carried it to the shelf, the tomb. I placed black cloth all around it and let it wait for light and hope.

The time of waiting between Good Friday and Easter morning took on a whole new dimension for me that year. Proclaiming "Alleluia" on Easter morning became an honest expression of God's faithfulness to me. In earlier years, I'd merely recited the liturgy, expressing a hope in something that might come, some day. And while the Easter acclamation has been and will always be a hope for the future, then "Alleluia" became a testimony to God's faithfulness in my life right now. I'd found a way to connect to the hard wood of the cross, to place my life there with God. In the process I'd found a way to participate in the crucifixion, not merely by putting my sins on God, but by seeing the grace and love of a God so faithful as to die for me. I finally realized that the Easter acclamation was not some in-your-face triumph but a broken Alleluia—a song of praise and thanksgiving—of compassion and mercy. I had found the way home.

Prayer Nine: Finding Your Cross

Time Required: 1–2 hours

Opening Prayer

Jesus, Son of God, show me the path of your cross that I might walk it with you. Amen.

Materials

- Modeling or firing potter's clay. The modeling clay is easiest to work with since it is cheap, forgiving, and widely available. However, it's a temporary form and you might want your work to be more enduring. Potter's clay is also easy to find and inexpensive but it can present technical challenges for a beginner. If you go this route, be sure to purchase terra cotta or raku clay and avoid porcelain; it can be quite difficult to work with and often cracks. It can also be difficult to find someone to fire potter's clay, but you usually can find a studio if you're diligent. You might also consider a newer self-hardening clay that most craft stores carry, such as Activa Air Dry. While more expensive, many of the technical and practical challenges go away with the ease of its use. You might try it first, and then if you find sculpting particularly rewarding, move on to potter's clay. Check with your area parks, recreation, and tourism office to see if a potter's studio is available. If so, you will not only find a studio to purchase tools, clay, and firings, you will also discover an inexpensive and fun space in which to work with others. Private studios and some ceramics shops also have space for beginners.
- Modeling tools, purchased specifically for use with clay, or odds and ends from your household and kitchen. Plastic forks, knives, and spoons, as well as seashells, pins, pencils, and other items make excellent tools for cutting and embossing.
- A board, preferably wooden, for your workspace. Remember to select a board large enough to accommodate your completed piece.

Prayer Method

- Find a worktable in a quiet environment.

- Arrange all your materials on the table and find a comfortable chair. You might cover the floor with newsprint or plastic and wear old clothing. Modeling clay can be messy and difficult to clean. Potter's clay is dusty but will almost always wash up well.
- Take time to acknowledge God's presence with you and thank God for the love you receive in God's faithfulness.
- If possible, spend twenty minutes or more in silence. You might consider picking a word or a simple phrase as your mantra, especially one that reminds you of the cross you're called to in God's life. Examples of possible prayers include simply the word "cross" or "suffering," or scriptural phrases such as "Surely this was the Son of God." If music appeals to you, you might listen to a recording of something like the spiritual "Were You There When They Crucified My Lord?"
- Let the mantra be your only prayer. If extraneous thoughts come your way, acknowledge them and then place them to the side. They will be there later if you need them. Use the techniques from the tips offered in Window Two (page 17) if the thoughts and critics really pester you.
- After spending time in silence and allowing your heart, mind, and soul to open to God, take the clay and begin to work it. Don't worry about the form or technical aspects of the work.
- Try to keep the design simple at first. As you repeat this exercise or work with clay more frequently, you'll gradually learn more advanced techniques. But this first time, just keep things simple. This first attempt can be a simple cross shape with or without a figure of Jesus on it.
- If an event or person from your journey comes to mind, imagine placing it on the surface of the clay and working it into your cross. If you like, you can sculpt a symbol or form that represents that thought and allow it to become a part of the cross you create. You can use two basic methods.

    First, you can imprint the symbol by pressing a tool into the clay, drawing it with a toothpick or needle tool, or using a natural object as a stamp.

    Second, you can create an independent piece and then attach it to the cross.

If you are using a modeling or self-hardening clay, use the push and pull method to incorporate the attachment. Push and pull the edges of the piece into the main body of the cross so that it is attached in both directions. When using potter's clay, this method works well with large attachments. Just be sure to use a prop to hold the attachment in place.

For smaller potter's clay attachments created independently, use a slip. A slip is a mixture of clay and water that forms a "glue" to attach the piece. Take a small amount of clay and mix in a few drops of water with your finger to form a paste. Use the paste between the pieces you are attaching.

- When you've finished, close your eyes and give thanks for the time you've enjoyed discovering more of God's faithfulness to you. Slowly open your eyes and let your gaze center on your crucifix. Don't be critical. Spend some time looking at what you've created to see what it has to say to you.

- If you need to address any technical issues with the sculpture, do so only after taking enough time to be with it. Generally, the following will guide you in getting the piece ready for drying and firing, if you desire to keep it.

  - Repair any cracks by making sure the clay is attached in both directions.

  - The clay should be no more than 1.5 inches thick. If you have a large mass of clay, find a way to hollow it out. Often, a piece can be hollowed from the bottom or from an area that won't be visible when the sculpture is fired. Use a needle tool to vent areas that are too narrow to hollow out any other way. For example, poke numerous spots underneath the piece so that air can escape during firing. Without using the needle tool, you run the risk of trapping air, which can cause cracks during firing.

  - With larger pieces that are too wet to hollow out upon completion, cover the piece with plastic. A simple grocery bag works very well. Check on the drying after about eight hours to see if it's ready for hollowing. Use a hollowing tool, available from most craft and art supply stores. It's ready to hollow when the exterior is starting to harden, but hasn't yet turned a lighter color. The exterior will still be somewhat malleable.

- If some areas are thin and others thick, consider wrapping thin areas with a damp paper towel and plastic to even out the drying process.
- Check out books on sculpture from your local library for more technical information.

Soul Questions

- How has the cross been a part of your journey thus far?
- What emotions did you experience during the exercise? What do those emotions have to say to you and your spiritual journey?
- What themes emerged in your prayer? How were they surprises to you?
- How does Jesus respond to your cross? What does Jesus say about the cross that you made? What words would Jesus use to describe it?
- What expectations did you bring to the cross? How are they different now that you've made your journey there?
- What challenges do you face as you move from the cross to the empty tomb?

Tools For the Journey

- Go on a field trip to area churches. Do they have a cross? What kind? What does it say about their life in Christ? What does it say about how they understand and live with Jesus?
- Go to the library and look at various travel and cultural magazines. Notice how many crosses you see in the photos. What do the crosses say to you about culture, people, and beliefs?
- Take a daytime walk in a downtown urban area. As you walk, what crosses do you see being borne by the people you encounter? Do you see homeless, destitute people bearing their crosses quite openly? Do you see people clutching their crosses so tightly that you can't really see them at all? Have you ever thought about others in such a way? Have you ever looked at others seeking their crosses?
- Make a list of all the crosses in your life. How have you held them tightly? How can you open them up to others and to God?

WINDOW TEN
Finding the Empty Tomb

*But on the first day of the week, at early dawn, they came to
the tomb, taking the spices that they had prepared. They
found the stone rolled away from the tomb, but when they
went in, they did not find the body. While they were perplexed
about this, suddenly two men in dazzling clothes stood beside
them. The women were terrified and bowed their faces to the
ground, but the men said to them, "Why do you look for the
living among the dead? He is not here, but has risen."*

Luke 24:1–5

The cross is not the end. It's the beginning.

The cross sets the passion of God in motion, and once God starts moving toward us, nothing—not even death—stops God. By taking on the pain
and suffering of our lives and sharing in our joys and triumphs, God shares
with us in the very life we've been given. Our God isn't some deity stuck in
heaven, separated from us and our sorrows, but a God who has been, is, and
will always be among us. Such love, presence, and faithfulness were so fully
expressed in the death of Christ that the cross—God's great self-portrait—
is the image that defines who God is. But the self-portrait is not limited to
the cross frozen on Good Friday. No, God's self portrait is a continuous
journey from the cross to the empty tomb. It is as if the cross of Good Friday
sets the form of the portrait while the sun of Easter morning sheds light on
it and gives it meaning.

All of us have experienced loss,—the kind that plunges us into darkness.
Sometimes, when we're lucky, the meaning of the experience comes into

focus quickly. Other times, it can take months or even years for the light to finally land on the cross we've borne. Recently, I was honored to see the light unfold quickly in the life of a woman in my former parish.

This incredible lady, who had suffered an aneurysm years earlier, had recovered to live a full and faithful life. A devoted mother and wife, she was an accomplished teacher and professor and everybody loved her dearly for her wit, humor, and strength. So when she was diagnosed with a rare syndrome that would claim her life quickly, we all wept.

But Betty kept right on going. Despite dark and bitter days when her memory would lapse, she never lost a sense of who she was. She always kept a glimmer in her eye, a smile on her face, and a gesture of love at hand. For some reason, this lady was able to push through the darkness to the light in one movement. There was something beyond her daily prayers, said faithfully. There was something greater than mere Scripture written in her heart. There was something in her being, some form of life as art that had helped her shape her life into the life that God had given. And that became clear the day she died.

As I sat in the hospital with her loving husband, we talked more about Betty. Her life, what she had done, the things she loved—all those things that filled her days with laughter and joy. But as we talked, I discovered something I didn't know. She'd spent years collecting seashells—not just a few, but more than you could count. She had a gracious English collector's cabinet at home, drawer after drawer full of perfect specimens of shells. But that wasn't all; there were buckets and baskets full of them in the garage. Betty had combed beaches for years, walking alone, spending hours looking at the shells, the little houses creatures had cast off to move on to another one. Within the lines, colors, curves, and twists of shells she'd found the incarnate life of prayer—an outward and visible sign of inward and spiritual grace. And so, a shell became the metaphor for her life. Dark days had come, days following the aneurysm, and the last weeks of her life, but could it be that she had so internalized the lessons of the shells that she was able to see through the darkness and into the light?

I think so, for her final prayer, a perfect art form in and of itself, was such a testimony. At her funeral, baskets of shells were placed at all the doors so that the congregation could take one as they left. She didn't just leave them there as a reminder of her life. Instead, she seemed to understand that the shell pointed to something greater. She knew deep within her soul that despite all the places we feel stranded, all the places where only the darkness of our cross is in view, light lies just ahead. For Betty, that light was found in gathering shells no matter what the weather of life, no matter what the storm, no matter what the season. Her life had shown us a way to see beyond the darkness and straight into the light—if we would only listen to the lesson of the shells.

Such is the message of the empty tomb. Whatever we've faced, God redeems. God reaches out and takes our sorrows, nails them to the tree, places them in the tomb, and waits with us for the light of Easter morning. In every child diagnosed with cancer, in every victim of violence, in every lonely widow, in every addiction, in every frustration and anxiety God is there working, loving, embracing. God is waiting for you and me to release whatever darkness claims us so that Christ can take it to the cross and then welcome the happy morning of Easter light. Our prayer becomes a question of what have we not given over to God, what we have withheld, what we have denied Christ to take to the cross. For when we admit what we have hidden, we turn that much more over to God. It is in that moment that Easter light shines into our darkness and the empty tomb shines upon us.

Prayer Ten: Pictures of Life and the Love of God

Time Required: 1 ½ hours

Opening Prayer

Christ, let love fill me with grace that all the dark places of my life might be resurrected and come to bask in your life and light. Amen.

Materials

- Assemble numerous photographs of your life. Be sure to collect a variety of photos from your childhood, teen years, and adult life. If you don't want to cut the photographs, take the ones you like and make copies. Black and white paper copies are just as useful as expensive color copies or reprints. Digital copies from your computer printer work well, as do photos from digital processing centers.
- A form upon which to glue your collage. For an inexpensive creation, use foam core. You might cut it into the shape of a cross, carefully using

a razor tool. You could also use heavyweight poster board. If you're a woodworker or know someone who is, you might make a pattern of a cross you like, trace it on plywood, and cut it out with a jigsaw. Some craft stores carry small wooden crosses, about two feet in height, during the Lenten season. Or consider using a small wooden box or heavyweight cardboard box to create Christ's tomb if you don't want to use a cross.

- Scissors, scrapbook photo cutters, or a knife tool.
- Glue. Be sure to use a base that will be compatible with the final finish.
- Varnish, polyurethane, or some other finish. Spray finishes work best with a paper or foam core base. Just follow product instructions and use multiple coats if possible.

Prayer Method

- Find a worktable in a quiet place.
- Arrange all your materials in front of you and sit in a comfortable chair.
- Take time to acknowledge God's presence with you and thank God for the protection you receive in God's faithfulness.
- Spend about twenty minutes in silence. You might consider picking a word or phrase as your mantra, as a simple prayer or reminder of the cross you're called to carry in God's life. Examples of possible prayers include simply the name "Jesus" or the word "suffering," or phrases such as "and they led him to the place of the skull and crucified him," or musical phrases such as "Were You There When They Crucified My Lord?"
- Let the mantra be your only prayer. If extraneous thoughts come your way, acknowledge them and then place them to the side. They will be there later if you're meant to address them. If they really pester you, write them down and place them aside.
- Begin to go through your pictures. If one of them speaks of the cross in your life, place it to the side for possible inclusion in the collage cross you'll make. In my own life, pictures from a difficult time in my life would be good examples. Or if we are grieving, a picture of the loved one that has died might be appropriate. Make a separate stack of any pictures that seem more like the empty tomb, such as birthday or holiday pictures with family and friends or a photo of a favorite pet from childhood.

- Once you've selected many pictures, begin to arrange those that reminded you of the cross along the inside of the form you've prepared. Try not to take too much time in selecting and arranging the photographs. Let them choose the spot they desire.
- Next, take the pictures that reminded you of the empty tomb and place them along the perimeter of the form. If you see relationships between the cross pictures and these, put them close together if you can.
- Using scissors or another cutting tool, cut the photographs and place them on the form. Be creative. You might burn the edges of the cross pictures and then make the empty tomb pictures more whimsical, using scrapbook scissors that create a fun edge.
- You may begin gluing the pictures when you're ready. Some people like to place everything before gluing; others glue as they go.
- When you're finished gluing, take the time to let God speak to you through your own life placed on the cross. Look for themes and trends in your composition. Consider the overall feeling and your emotions at having been so honest with God.
- As a final step, finish the piece with several layers of polyurethane or spray lacquer, making sure your glue and the finish are compatible. Several light coatings are much better and more effective than using heavy coatings.

Soul Questions

- What images of the cross do you see throughout your life? How do these crosses surprise you?
- What images of the empty tomb do you see throughout your life? Why have you sometimes failed to notice the times when God was resurrecting life around you?
- How does it feel to have such an intimate identification with Christ on the cross as a part of your spiritual journey? What about in sharing the empty tomb? How does it feel to share in the resurrection?
- How have this exercise and all the prayers of this book helped you to contemplate the hope of your own resurrection?
- What kind of bumper sticker would you create at the end of these exercises? What one- or two-word phrase describes your prayer life after going through the exercises?

- How are you making prayer a daily practice?
- What obstacles remain in your prayer life?
- What new artistic exercises might you plan to deepen your prayer method?

Tools for the Journey

- What would your Easter Day be like? What would you do? Write a poem or description of it. You might not be able to do it all, but you can probably accomplish at least a part of it. Treat yourself to your Easter Day.
- Plan an Easter feast. Celebrate your life with those dear to you by having a festive dinner party.
- Go into a dark room and sit there in meditation for an extended period. When you have presented all you can before God, light a candle and let the light fill the room. Reflect on the presence of light amidst darkness. How can you take the image of such light into your daily life?
- What would it be like to dance with God? Imagine you can by painting, sculpting, or acting it out.

THE OPEN WINDOW
The Final Medium

For God so loved the world that he gave his only Son, so that everyone who believes in him may not perish but may have eternal life.

John 3:16

Through prayer and art, we've opened ten spiritual windows. As we've jumped into the prayer exercises, we've discovered more about who we are—and in the process we've found ourselves resting in the loving arms of the risen Christ. Of course, none of us is really good at praying. Perhaps we're not supposed to be. Instead, we have sought a way to make the discipline real, honest, and most important, daily. If we keep working at it, the life of prayer will begin to live within and without us—our empty vessels will fill with God's grace and the life we seek inwardly will be lived outwardly. In this symbiotic relationship between the inner and outer life our souls awaken from their slumber and we discover the joyful dance of the soul's journey. Such a place of joy is a place of acceptance—a place where we've seen both the abyss and the apex, the light and the darkness, the horrors and the happiness that our life brings. Indeed, it's in such a place that we feel God's outstretched arms holding us and we begin to dance.

In my own journey, the music for the dance came a couple of years after the death of Molly and Abbie. Just after being ordained to the priesthood, I met William. At eighteen, he was tall, handsome, and perceptive, with incredibly wise eyes and big, strong hands. He could wear a hat better than any teenager I knew and tie-dyed shirts—well, they looked like black tuxedos on him. He had what it takes to love life and have life love you.

He also had cancer.

Over the course of the next two years, I talked to William many times. At first, our conversations on the phone were very much the priest and the young man. I would call. He would be nice. I would mention the weather. He would say something about the sun, clouds, or rain. We would talk about who had come to visit or what the doctor said he needed to do next. Sometimes, William would talk about the future, whether he would resume college, and whether he would ever meet that special girl. But he said very little about how he felt. He said a lot about how others felt. He was always more worried about them.

I kept calling, thinking all the while that he really didn't want me to, but knowing that he understood why I did. At one point, I thought one of his parents would tell me to stop calling. After all, parents who face cancer in their only child should feel anger and resentment toward God, or, for that matter, toward a minister. I think I would. But they never said to stop. There were weeks, even months, when we didn't actually say a lot, but through cards and calls, we kept in touch.

After about a year, William called me one day. By that time, he was nineteen, but his soul was much older and wiser. The disease was taking a physical toll and his body began to feel and look like that of an older man. The tall, lanky build of this great golfer was becoming crippled, torn, bruised, and dejected. But the other trait of age was also coming his way. He was acquiring the deep wisdom that comes quickly when you see life as it is, look death in the face, and stare at God eye to eye.

And so, when William called that day he talked and talked. He said a great deal about his mother—how sad she was, and how very happy he wanted her to be. And as painful as it was, he talked about his father—how they shared golf, how they could just be with each other, not saying a word, but knowing fully what the other was thinking, hoping, and dreaming. He voiced his concern about how his parents would live without him. He was their only child, and he knew he was not supposed to die first.

In other calls to me, he began to talk openly about his disease. Early on, he'd never talked directly about it. He might have mentioned it but he usually danced around it, bringing up only his medication or treatment. Actually discussing the disease, and using the word "cancer" weren't his style. But now, he would cuss about this cancer in him, using words he said "priests aren't supposed to hear." He'd tell me how the disease looked to him—its dark colors, hazy boundaries, and claw-like grasps reaching throughout his body. And in the process, William began to open more and more of his soul to God and to me. I could see that despite the cancer, William was climbing ever so slowly up the edge of his abyss.

A few months later, on a cold December day, the phone rang yet again. I didn't expect to hear the poetry of William's soul taking flight on the other end as he opened its windows. But that's what I heard. It was as if in one moment he stood on the bottom of the abyss, on solid ground, railing against God, revealing the deepest and darkest desires of his soul, purging it of all his possessions. "You know, don't you, I don't want to die," he said when I picked up the phone. "I want to be here for a long, long time. I want to be with my parents, see new things with them—hell, just go to the beach with them. I want to screw up and laugh about it in years to come. I want to drink, smoke, and eat it all so I can taste and see all that the world has to offer. I want to fall in love again and again, and one day, have children. I want to see my Dad play his best round of golf ever and I want to dance with my Mom on my wedding day. Damn it. Damn you. I don't want to die."

And then silence as I cried, sitting there holding the phone to my ear, not willing to let go of the conversation, that incredible window into William's soul. He had opened the window—all the windows—wide open, wider than I'd ever seen. And despite my tears, despite his, I knew that we both could see the light coming in. William had let it out. Completely depleted of physical strength, he'd tapped into a spiritual freedom that was so powerful because it was all that was left. By telling God off, indeed by cursing God, William had pushed through to a new level. He'd found a song, a lament that he sang with Christ, screaming from his cross, "My God, my God. Why have you forsaken me?" And more importantly, he'd pushed through that song to the other side, a place of total dispossession, a place of letting go, a place of belovedness. The cancer was going to kill his body, but the spirit was going to liberate William's soul. He had told God off. He had let God have it. And there was nothing more to say. The light was shining in the darkness and the darkness had not overcome it.

From that moment William's soul took flight within a body that was withering away. I'd never watched someone as young as William die. Abbie's and Molly's deaths had been sudden, terrifying from their very unexpectedness. William's death was slow, horrifying from its very inevitability. And yet, because I'd witnessed William opening the windows to his soul in the process of dying, William's death brought grace to all our deaths. In seeing William live his life fully and in watching the windows to his soul open, I was sure all God's children could ultimately see through to the other side.

The days before William's death were like looking directly into heaven— even if they did feel more like hell. On my last visit to William, he was lying in his bed. By now his whole room was a creative icon, a holy space, something through which to see God. With the help of his friends, his room had been decorated with the images of William's life. Posters, photo collages, ceramic mosaics, a cross a friend had made, a small pottery bowl—you name it, it was there. All the lovely prayers of William's life were on display, like an art installation in a fine gallery.

Music was blasting as I walked into the room. One of William's friends was there visiting. He jumped up upon seeing me, a priest with collar and all walking in, and rushed to the stereo to turn down the volume. William's hollow cheeks just chuckled as he said, "He can handle it. He knows this is the stuff God listens to." And there, in the room of a twenty-year-old just a day away from death, I began to see the wholeness of William's prayer. I could see that William and his friends had created a place of love, a place where the innermost thoughts of a young man dying of cancer could be cast on the wall of his room, the canvas of his life. I could see William as a child—joyous, happy, ecstatic. I could see the fear in his eyes as an early teen, captured in icons of collage. And then, the images, art, the prayers all gave way and I could see more than William. I could see all the hosts of heaven, Abbie and Molly included, surrounding his bed as they sang right along with the sounds of Van Morrison blaring from the stereo.

The next morning, William died in his mother's arms. Three days later, in the nave of a grand and glorious church, William brought the melody of the cross and the dance of the empty tomb right before our eyes. With all the icons of his life gathered in the church —collages, photos, scrapbooks, and posters—a band began playing Van Morrison's "Have I Told You Lately That I Love You." And hearing the call of the empty tomb, William's mother stood gently in her pew, wrapped her arms around herself, and danced. William had gotten what he wanted—to dance with his mom.

It was a masterpiece.

Now, God calls you to the life of Christ, the dance that William, with Abbie, Molly, and all the saints, invites us to. They ask you to turn over all the places you've hidden from God and in so doing to let God's light shine in the midst of your darkness. For the saints know what we have yet to learn— that openness, honesty, and vulnerability before God are the keys to finding love and freedom in this life and in the life to come. So, scribble, get paint in your hair, and dance wildly with excitement, for God is ready to see you face to face. Indeed, that's all that God desires—for your eyes to behold the eyes of Christ, the eyes of the one who says, I love you.

Appendix

Small-Group Study

While this book is written for the individual, it is easily adaptable for small groups. Individuals could covenant to do the exercises at home and then come together to share what each learned in the process. The soul questions can serve as a guide for such discussions. Other groups are comfortable coming together in quietness and working in community as each exercise is explored. Such an arrangement might provide the accountability that so many of us need for a life of prayer. Practically, it also makes the process easier. By pooling supplies and resources, there's less work and expense involved in preparation. There's also something rather powerful about the studio experience—the energy of working independently yet in community.

The following exercise provides such groups the opportunity to share in one guided prayer together. It takes a good bit of planning but is well worth the effort.

First, the group selects a facilitator for the process. If possible, invite a trusted person from outside the group. You might consider inviting a member of the clergy or a spiritual director; people trained in pastoral counseling are usually better choices than a spouse or friend, although those are possible.

Invite the group to assemble, asking them *not to read beyond the materials section that follows*. The process depends on the use of the facilitator and the participants' lack of knowledge about the process. Don't succumb to the temptation to read the prayer beforehand. Doing so will spoil the process for you and the group. You must use a facilitator.

Group Prayer

Time Required: About 1 hour

Materials

Each participant needs a small piece of modeling clay. You can use fireable clay or the typical modeling clay found in most craft stores. A small bag of fireable potter's clay would be enough for eight to twelve people to complete the exercise.

Prayer Method

Only the facilitator should read beyond this point.

The following is a script for leading two or more participants through this exercise. During the exercise, participants should remain silent. Your function is to create a non-anxious, reassuring atmosphere of trust by carefully following the instructions. Don't deviate from the supplied text and follow all instructions carefully. Be sure to read slowly and avoid rushing the process. Embrace silence throughout, especially when a pause is indicated. Italicized items are for your information and are not to be read aloud.

Script for Facilitator

Arrange the participants in chairs, seated in a circle.
- Sitting in the circle, place both feet on the floor, hold the clay in your hands without moving it, and close your eyes.
- Take a deep breath in, and then slowly out.
- Take another deep breath in, and then slowly out.
- Keep your eyes closed as you thank God for this time and for the chance to learn more about yourself and about your relationship with God.

Pause.
- Begin moving the clay back and forth between your hands, forming a sphere. Remember to keep your eyes closed. As distractions come your way, place them on the clay in your imagination and continue to pass the clay back and forth between your hands.

Pause.

- Notice how the clay feels. Notice how it is warm and yet cold. Soft and yet hard. Weak and yet strong.

Pause.

- In just a moment, I will give you a word upon which to meditate. When I give you that word, begin to work the clay. If an image comes to mind, begin working it into the clay. If an image does not come to mind, just continue working without any idea of the direction in which you journey. But remember to keep your eyes closed.

- If possible, work with your non-dominant hand. So, if you are left-handed, use your right hand; if you are right-handed, use your left hand. After I give you the word upon which to meditate, we will enter a period of silence during which you will work in the clay. When you are finished, just hold the clay in your hands, keeping your eyes closed.

Pause.

- The word that I give you is "trust."

Pause. In most cases, the participants will work for ten to fifteen minutes. If they go longer, that is fine. Proceed when they appear finished.

- Now, keeping your eyes closed, take your hands and feel the creation that you hold. Notice how it feels—its texture, shape and overall emotion. Take time with it.

Pause for a minute or two.

- In a minute, I'm going to ask you to do something with the clay. At first, you might not want to, but just let go of any inhibitions and let the process work its way out. No one will embarrass you and no one will have to say anything after the exercise. Just trust the process.

- Open your eyes. How does the object look to you now? Is it the same as when you felt it only with your hands? How do you respond?

Pause for a minute or two.

- And now, going with the process, take your creation and pass it to the person on your left. Once you give yours and receive that of another, immediately close your eyes.

- Do not move the clay you hold. Only skim it with your fingers.

- How does it feel to hold someone else's trust?

Pause.

- Does the creation have any similarities with what you have made?

Pause.
- How is it different?

Pause.
- How do you identify with it? Take a minute or two to reflect on how this creation, this part of another, feels.

Pause.
- Return the object to its owner.

Pause.
- Compare how it now feels to hold your creation again after someone else has touched it. Is it the same? Different? How so? Did you feel vulnerable while someone else held your clay? How about your piece? Were you worried that someone touching it would ruin it?

Pause.
- Close your eyes once again.
- Give thanks to God for what you have discovered of your self and how trust looks or feels to you.

Pause.
- Give thanks to God for experiencing the trust of another and for the willingness of a fellow companion to share.
- Amen.

Soul Questions
- What experiences have formed your feelings about trust? Who has disappointed you so much that you failed to trust them? Who could you always rely on in your life?
- How might those experiences have impacted your relationship with God?
- What does it take for you to trust another person?
- What does it take for you to trust God?
- What images came to mind when you were meditating and working the clay?
- What was it like to hear you'd be passing your creation to another person?
- What was it like to receive your creation back?
- What did the prayer reveal that you need to address before trusting God and others more?

Preparing for Individual Confession

The self-portrait exercises, along with all the other prayers, have taken our prayers deeper. Now you may choose to take the additional step of going to a minister or spiritual director who takes the role of confessor. If so, there are several steps that might make the process less daunting and at the same time more enlightening. While the journey into the sacrament or act of confession can be riddled with twists and turns, the reward is clear—actually hearing another human being say that you are a loved and forgiven child of God.

Find a confessor.

First, find a confessor you trust. If you don't trust the person, you might as well not go. Most people are comfortable going to their minister or a spiritual director but sometimes it is helpful to find a person that will just serve as your confessor. Consider going on a retreat to a monastic community and as part of that time confessing your sins to a brother or sister there. Don't be concerned if your faith tradition doesn't include monasteries. If I were guessing, a majority of people who visit them for retreat are from another tradition. Or ask your minister or friends if they know a spiritual director in a neighboring city or town. I go a couple of hours away from my community for confession. Something about going to another place creates a sense of trust and creates a safe boundary. If you find someone you have not previously known, visit first and develop trust before the confession.

Go slowly.

Take the time to reflect upon life and how you may have injured others. Reflection upon the sin in life allows you to consider how those sins grieved the heart of God. This step is often the most difficult. Take the time to listen to the screaming silence of God as you consider how your actions have thwarted God's love and grace in this world. We most often realize how we have affected others but rarely do we actually consider how we have failed ourselves.

Confession is not a laundry list.

Remember that you need not recall every single sin in infinite detail. You cannot. You will not. Confession brings honesty before God. It is not to create an exhaustive inventory of your worst moments in life. When you begin such a process, it is easy to be overwhelmed and to start to think that you will never be able to identify all the sin in your life, and that can be depressing. But the realization that you will never purge all sin is the beginning of grace—grace upon grace, mercy upon mercy.

Recall specifics to go deeper.

You can no doubt remember times that you have failed to treat another person as a child of God. We do it each day. But to dig down deep and honestly say that you acted that way because you are full of pride is another. Or worse, to admit that you categorize people and discount them because of where they are from, where they went to school or what color their skin is; that is a deep sin within everyone, a sin rarely addressed yet desperately in need of confession. Remembering the incident, the person or the event can lead to the root of sin and the hope of transformation and renewal down deep, not just on the surface.

Encounter confession as a gift.

You might dread it or loathe it as I did. It can seem so severe. And yet, it is a blessed gift. God gives confession as a way to remember our humanity and the gift of it from God as Creator. In it you can discover a pathway toward honesty and forgiveness. When you discover that place, you will find yourself resting in God and trusting in God's faithfulness to you. And so when you address confession as a gift to be unwrapped and discovered, the weariness passes and you find liberation.

Allow confession to bring peace.

Harboring feelings, especially negative thoughts, fears and anxieties, encourages the creation of a sphere of combat within the soul. Lacking honesty in our lives, countless hours can be spent thrashing about in the wrongs committed because we cannot rest in the peace of God's faithfulness. We begin constructing webs of explanation and self-justification. We indulge in certainty and over-rationalize everything from behavior to doctrine. We match our fears with an inflated sense of self. We substitute our opinion for reasoned choice. We confuse ourselves by living in the lies of the world and discounting the promises of a God we cannot see. Confession opens all these things up to God and ushers in peace. Opening your heart to God, you let God's stillness invade your life and drive from it all these misdirected attempts toward wholeness. You gain peace because you go to God honestly and in candid words, sighs, tears, and laughter you find your soul resting before God, in God, among God's people.

Confession saves us.

Being saved is such a trite phrase in most religion today. It is a tired, overused, misunderstood and squandered term that hardly addresses an honest journey with God. But confession literally saves us from ourselves as it restores the whole person to the rightful place as a creature of God's own making, God's own choosing. When you find the peace of God in confession, you find it because you're reminded of who you are and whose you are. When you get honest, you remember that you were formed from the dust of the earth, in God's image and likeness. You remember that God redeemed you and was faithful in Jesus Christ, and like the prodigal son coming home, rediscover belovedness in a God who treasures your every breath.

You are not alone.

Being saved from ourselves also means being surrounded by a great cloud of witnesses who have run the race set before them. As some of the older services for confession said, "I have squandered the inheritance of your saints." Confession reminds not only of the need for honesty before God but also of honesty's place with all those who have gone before us. The saints who have walked this earth committed the same sins, the same terrible mistakes, and the same turnings away from God and God's ways. Saints celebrated in the Church, indeed the major characters of the faith, Abraham, Sarah, Peter and Paul, all committed the same sins that you and I do. Just look at the opening pages of the Bible. Disobedience, stealing, murder, hatred, and idolatry are all there. Whatever we have done is there. But more important, and more essential, is a faithful God that leads and preserves in spite of it. Faithful servants confess their faults to God, sometimes before calamity, sometimes after it. But rest assured that the saints before us committed the same sins and God's grace was sufficient.

Confession is coming home.

As the rite of honesty with God, it is the prodigal turning around and heading back to his place in the world. It is facing up to the inheritance and brushing off our clothes once again, only to realize the baptismal garment and the kingdom have been there all along. It is saying, "I am sorry. I messed up. Forgive me." And likewise, with all the heavenly hosts, it is hearing God's voice saying, loud and clear, "Welcome home. Bring a robe. Kill the fatted calf. Eat, drink and make merry. For this child of mine who was lost is found. This child has come home."

Art and Spirituality
Books from Morehouse

Knitting into the Mystery:
A Guide to the Shawl-Knitting Ministry
by Susan S. Jorgensen and Susan S. Izard

"Fans of knitting will be, shall we say, hooked: the book offers practical steps on selecting yarn and knitting simple prayer shawls, but its most enduring feature is the heartwarming stories of shawls knitted and given as artifacts of prayer." —*Publishers Weekly*

"This is an awe-inspiring book about a very meaningful spiritual practice. . . . In a time when spiritual practices are expanding in so many fascinating and special ways, this is an essential volume for church libraries. For as the authors of Knitting into the Mystery put it, our hands are God's hands." —*Spirituality & Health*

"Those readers familiar with reading about spiritual matters will find the book inspiring. For those thinking of starting a shawl-knitting ministry in their community, this book may offer the needed motivation." —*Creative Knitting Magazine*

Coming Soon
from Morehouse

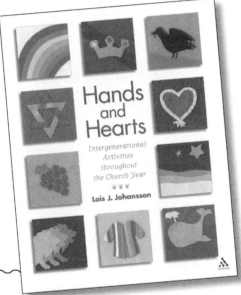

Hands and Hearts:
Intergenerational Activities
throughout the Church Year

by Lois J. Johansson

A source of fun and biblical learning, *Hands and Hearts* is a great way to draw together a congregation of all ages for spiritual growth and learning. This interactive book includes easy-to-follow instruction for activities, based on the liturgical year, designed to help your church family experience faith-based learning together.

Available May 2006

COMING SOON
from Morehouse

Fabric of Faith:
A Guide to the
Prayer Quilt
Ministry
by Kimberly Winston

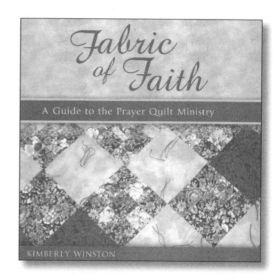

For countless generations, patchwork quilts have been a visible act of love. Pieced together from bits and pieces of material, they represent the handiwork and devotion of the quilter—and a deep and comforting connection with the person they're presented to.

Fabric of Faith is the story of the Prayers and Squares ministry. It chronicles the amazing ways Prayers and Squares has touched lives and hearts around the world, and offers directions and patterns for making quilts and starting a parish or community chapter. Author Kimberly Winston rounds it out with a selection of prayers, written from many faith traditions, to offer with each complete quilt.

Available June 2006